Paranormal

Paranormal
LONDON

NEIL ARNOLD

The
History
Press

This book is dedicated to Jemma, with love

First published 2010

The History Press
The Mill, Brimscombe Port
Stroud, Gloucestershire, GL5 2QG
www.thehistorypress.co.uk

British Library Cataloguing in Publication Data.
A catalogue record for this book is available from the British Library.

ISBN 978 0 7524 5591 4

Typesetting and origination by The History Press
Printed in Great Britain
Manufacturing managed by Jellyfish Print Solutions Ltd

CONTENTS

ACKNOWLEDGEMENTS

I would like to thank the following for their help in the production of this book:

My parents, Ron and Paulene; my sister Vicki; my nan and granddad, Ron and Win; my girlfriend, Jemma; Londonist; Joe Chester; Terry Cameron; David Farrant; Jonathan Downes and all at The Centre for Fortean Zoology; London Paranormal; Jason Day; The London Word; Jacqui Ford; Karl Shuker; Nick Redfern; Chris Eades; *Fortean Times*; Alan Friswell; *Time Out*; The Natural History Museum; Adam Smith; all the newspapers mentioned within and all the witnesses who came forward to tell their stories.

All photographs are copyright of Neil Arnold.

FOREWORD

London is teeming with paranormal phenomena. Even as I write, there comes a report of a UFO, a glowing orange ball of light, seen over Streatham Common. It would appear that UFOs sighted in London are not exclusive to desolate Streatham Common; several reports have come in over the years from people who claim to have seen 'strange objects' or small craft in the skies over Hampstead Heath and a dedicated group of UFO researchers meet regularly on the Heath, in the hope of obtaining some definite photographic evidence.

One of London's most misunderstood yet sinister ghosts resides in Highgate Cemetery. It is said by some to have been a vampire, although generally it has been reported as being a more 'mundane' ghost – not withstanding the reports that it had 'hypnotic red eyes'. I saw this figure myself at the end of 1969, as I was passing the top gate of the cemetery. So real did it first appear that I assumed it was a genuine person bent on frightening the odd passer-by. But when it suddenly vanished, without apparent cause, I was convinced I had witnessed something supernatural.

Highgate Cemetery has always been a mysterious place that closely guards its esoteric secrets. It is a fact that in the late 1960s a group of practicing Satanists were actually using the place to carry out their clandestine rituals. In 1971 I discovered the remains of one of their ceremonies in an isolated vault that they had broken into. Satanic signs adorned the marble floor of this small mausoleum, surrounded by the burnt-down stubs of black candles. For the record I took a photograph; this was to cause me trouble as it was later found by the police, who assumed that I had been personally responsible for this vandalism, and charged me accordingly.

Paranormal London provides a definitive account of varied psychic phenomena in the London area whose appearances may shock and even astound you. Neil Arnold, author of two best-selling books, *Monster! The A-Z of Zooform Phenomena*, and *Mystery Animals of the British Isles: Kent*, has long been a dedicated full-time investigator, who from the age of ten has avidly collected cuttings on ghosts and monsters from all over the country. He believes that serious research can only be done 'on the ground', and here he presents findings where fact takes precedence over unqualified fiction.

David Farrant, President of the British Psychic and Occult Society, 2010

INTRODUCTION

London has long been considered one of the most haunted places in the world, a city rich in history and culture, harbouring bizarre stories of sinister spectres and ghost-infested buildings. However, it can also boast a plethora of paranormal phenomena, from reports of large, exotic cats prowling the leafy suburbs to spine-chilling tales of monsters said to lurk in London's serpentine Underground. Herein is a veritable feast of uncanny, atmospheric yarns pertaining to flying serpents, UFOs, demons, spectral animals and all manner of bewildering riddles which we classify as 'paranormal'. While some of the contents may well be baffling though not completely bereft of solution, some of the stories told are never likely to reveal their truth.

So, light a candle, take a corner and remember that, although you may be but 5ft away from a rat at all times in the capital, you're also never far away from a ghost or strange creature either!

Neil Arnold, 2010

ONE

BEASTS IN OUR BACKYARDS

The 'alien big cat' mystery has peppered British folklore for at least two centuries. During the 1980s the so-called 'Beast of Exmoor' made the national papers as an alleged savage, livestock-slaughtering creature said to resemble a 'panther' that was roaming the West Country. The Royal Marines were called into action after there had been several eyewitness reports of an animal said to measure over 4ft in length, muscular in appearance and with a long, curving tail. Not since Sir Arthur Conan Doyle's *The Hound of the Baskervilles* novel had such a fear been instilled in the hearts and minds of ordinary folk. Then, in the 1990s, a new 'beast' emerged on the horizon; the 'Beast of Bodmin' was the name on everyone's lips, the media had a field-day, documentaries were made devoted to the pursuit of the animal, and arguments continued as to whether the fens and quagmires could support the alleged monster.

A majority of eyewitness reports described a big, black or fawn-coloured cat with a very long tail. Such details confused the press, who didn't know their panther from their leopard or their lynx from their puma. Other reports spoke of greyish-mottled cats with large, tufted ears and short stubby tails. While some sightings were evidently just large feral cats or dogs or foxes, there was indeed a consistency suggesting that puma, black leopard and lynx were indeed at large in the British Isles and soon, every county would have its mystery cat. The question the experts couldn't answer was how they got there. The lynx was native to the United Kingdom up until a few thousand years ago, but leopards and lions died out many thousands of years ago, while the puma had never been part of our woodlands.

The wooded areas of the United Kingdom are seemingly alive with large cats – and so are the concrete jungles of the capital!

The Surrey Puma

The Surrey Puma was the first mystery cat to make waves across England in the press. For many researchers this particular beast was pivotal in attracting the attention of the media and putting 'big cats' on the map in the country. Indeed, the first mention of a Surrey beast actually came centuries before the West Country was besieged by cat scratch fever.

The most quoted reference to an early 'beast' sighting around Surrey came from the pen of naturalist William Cobbett, in his *Rural Rides*. It is said that as a boy he observed a grey cat as big as a middle-sized spaniel dog while visiting Waverley Abbey, sometime between 1766 and 1770. On 27 October 1825 he took his eleven-year-old son to the exact same spot where he'd seen the animal. Many have suggested that Cobbett saw a wildcat (a cat now confined to the Scottish Highlands), while others have argued that he may well have observed a lynx.

The wildcat, now confined to Scotland. Did naturalist William Cobbett observe such a cat in Surrey or was it something bigger?

During the 1930s, a magazine known as *The Field* mentioned another early Surrey Puma encounter. It involved a lady named Irene Roberts, who, during the early hours of a July day, heard the most eerie cries close to her home at Lightwater. Irene wrote a letter to *The Field* a year later and described the cries as, '… of peculiar intensity, expressing, it seemed, mortal fear and physical pain.' Had she heard a large, elusive cat such a puma (which is known for its piercing scream) or simply not recognised the moans of a fox, even though she was used to such native calls?

In 1955 at Abinger Hammer, Surrey, a woman walking her dog stumbled across the remains of a calf. Naturally, the witness was shocked by her grisly find, but she was even more stunned when she saw what animal had killed the calf: a large gingery-coloured cat that sprang from the undergrowth and bounded away. A similar encounter took place four years later in the Hampshire area, but the most unusual report came from a taxi driver who, during the same year, reported seeing a lion near Tweseldown Racecourse in Hampshire.

The year 1963 was certainly the year of the beast and sightings persisted of a graceful cat, with a relatively small head, muscular shoulders and long, sweeping tail. Two years before, at Croham Golf Course in Surrey, a large black animal was spotted by a golfer as the autumnal mists descended over the greens. Police officers suggested the animal may have been a large dog and the witness felt he'd seen a bear, but is there a possibility that such an animal was in fact the Surrey Puma?

The puma (*felis concolor*) is at home in the dense woods of California. Despite its size (it is capable of reaching over 5ft in length), the puma is the largest of the 'lesser cats' and not technically a 'big cat', for it cannot roar like the lion, leopard, jaguar and tiger. It is also known as a mountain lion or cougar and is a fawn/tan-coloured cat with a white underside. Therefore, despite countless reports in the 1960s of a *black* puma, there is no evidence whatsoever to suggest that such animals exist. Reports of large, black cats would most certainly have concerned the melanistic (having dark, almost black coats due to a skin pigment known as melanin) form of the leopard. The 'black panther' is exactly the same animal as the black leopard or black jaguar. A 'panther' is not a species of cat, merely a term to describe melanistic leopards or jaguars.

If a big cat does indeed roam the Surrey countryside, how did it come to be there? Did it escape from a zoo or a private collection? Such escapees may not have been common, but they certainly would have happened over the course of history, and a now defunct website, under the heading 'Scare Bears & Other Creatures', was quick to highlight such escapees, writing:

In the 1920s Carmo Manor in Shirley acted as the winter quarters of Carmo's Circus. The Great Carmo's menagerie was housed there, and the circus men would often wash the elephants in the old estate pond or take bears for exercise around the grounds. So when a woman rang the police station to report an escaped leopard the duty sergeant was on the point of organising a full-scale, armed leopard hunt. The creature had been seen to force its way through a hedge and then jump over a fence. Stopping a moment to check the facts, he rang Carmo's and found they had no leopards! This time, the twilight at dusk was accused of turning a Dalmatian into a vision of a leopard. The circus dog had apparently slipped out during training for a new act.

The 1960s was a time when it was fashionable to have novelty pets such as big cats and it is possible that some of these may well have escaped, or been released, into the wild.

Strangely, not many reports of normal 'spotted' leopards have come to light, which confused many. But this can be explained. Black leopards (which still have rosettes evident under their dark coat) were ideal pets as cubs and any released/escaping into the countryside, either singularly or as pairs, would seek out members of the opposite sex (which must surely have existed in the British wilds otherwise such cats would simply have died out and no further reports would have been recorded). Black leopard pairs only spawn black offspring, hence sightings only of black cats locally. Although melanism occurs in other cats, such as the jaguar or bobcat, there is no evidence to suggest that jaguars are on the loose in the UK; such cats were not commonly kept as pets, and melanism appears rare in reference to other cat species sighted in Britain.

The 1980s noticed a huge lull in sightings of the Surrey Puma, despite rumour that a large black cat had been shot dead not far from Greenwich Observatory in London and the fact

Harrods Department Store at Knightsbridge. In the 1960s exotic cats could be purchased here.

that hair samples taken from Peaslake in Surrey were proven to originate from a large wild cat. Instead, there was a surge in reports from the West Country as the Exmoor Beast went on the rampage, and it would be this neck of the woods which would produce the most sightings over the next two decades; the so-called Surrey Puma was relegated to a mere whisper on the wind as the millennium dawned.

The Shooters Hill Cheetah

Lorry driver Mr David Back reported seeing an animal laying by the roadside at 1 a.m. on 18 July 1963, at Shooters Hill, south-east London. Thinking it may have been an injured dog, he decided to pull over and approach the animal. As he neared it, he realised that it was in fact a very large cat eating something. The cat sensed the approaching witness and bounded away. One hundred and twenty-six policemen, accompanied by more than twenty dogs, alongside ambulance staff and officials from the RSPCA, boy scouts and members of the public, scoured several acres of land in the hunt for a cat they believed was a cheetah. They found nothing – although it was alleged that a large cat-like animal sprang over the bonnet of one police vehicle.

A snarling cat was heard at Kidbrooke Sports Ground on 23 July, and once again a ridiculous number of policemen turned up, but their pursuit was fruitless. The cheetah hunters soon gave up their search.

The only reason that the cat was described as a cheetah was due to the fact that not even a police motorcycle, travelling at 70mph, could flush the animal out. In 2002, at Oxleas Wood, Shooters Hill, even a sighting of a big, black cat (most definitely a leopard) brought back the 'cheetah' headline. Yet, looking back on the legendary spate of sightings, it's clear that not on any occasion was a cheetah-like animal described or indeed seen.

In 1964 the sightings of a mystery cat escalated. Loxwood, Puttenham, Witley and Elstead were scenes of cat activity and these places were visited again in 1965 and '66 by possibly the same cat, or cats. Press interest had waned, but when a flurry of calls bombarded the news desk

During the 1960s it was rumoured that a cheetah was on the loose around London.

the hunt was back on … and then interest diminished once again. And so the saga continued, running its course, dying its death, being resurrected, and then fading, time and time again, just like the elusive predator in the Surrey woodlands.

> While I was out riding in Granger's Woods, Woldingham, in May 1978, I saw what I believe was a lion rush across the road in front of me. It ran from the Oxted side into thick bushes on the opposite side. It was about ten or twelve yards from me. It was a beige/light brown colour and had a small head in comparison with the rest of its body. (It had no shaggy mane).

So wrote eyewitness Anne Stanette after her encounter in east Surrey over a decade after the original reports. Again a lion was mentioned, although it is more likely to have been a puma mistaken for a lioness.

A Man Walks into a Pub …

The South Harrow Puma was owned by a man who, in 1974, often walked his prized pet through the local streets. However, during the November of that year, things got out of control. The owner in question casually strolled into the Farm House pub with his puma on a lead. After a short while several locals began to feel uncomfortable in the presence of the wild animal and so the man was asked to leave. Although he complied with the requests of the staff and customers, the beast didn't and went berserk. The landlady at the time commented that, 'It took the man fifteen minutes to get the puma out of the pub and into his car, during which it tore off the man's glove and ripped open his hand.' It also caused severe damage to the chair upholstery in the public house, as well as damaging tables, smashing glasses and demolishing the bar in its frenzy.

When the cat decided to shred the car seats the police were called to the scene, where, after a short time, they towed both the vehicle and the aggravated felid away. Later, the man was charged with being drunk and incapable. What happened to his cat was not recorded.

In 1975 a strange incident occurred at Acton, west London, when an estranged husband dumped his puma in the back garden of his former home, leaving his wife and kids trapped inside and screaming for help. The man left a note saying that he had nowhere else to put the cat. It took the local police and RSPCA two hours to get the terrified family out of the house.

The Tiger of Edgware

Edgware resident David Corbel awoke one August morning in 1988, peered from his kitchen window and, to his horror, saw an 8ft long cat perched on the branches of a tree in a neighbour's garden.

'I thought I was still dreaming, so I called my wife,' David commented at the time. 'She confirmed what I was seeing – it had a black body, ginger hindquarters and white paws.'

There is no large cat species which has this colouration. The melanistic leopard has a dark, seemingly black, coat that could appear gingery in sunlight, but they do not have white paws (although the paw pads could appear pale in comparison to coat colour), unless it had been standing in chalk or walked through paint!

Was a tiger sighted in Edgware?

It was reported that large paw-prints said to belong to the elusive animal were found in an area where a tree had been deeply scored, a marking sign of a large cat. However, despite a search, no trace of the animal was to be found. Some theorised that the cat had escaped from a circus that had been visiting the North London suburb.

The Lioness of Winchmore Hill

North London is hardly big cat country, but, during the early part of 1994, particularly around the Winchmore Hill area, several witnesses insisted they'd seen a cat resembling a lioness.

Linda Bostock had her sighting of the Winchmore Beast in broad daylight on 11 March, in the vicinity of Firs Lane, which runs parallel to the A10. She described the cat, which was walking along the canal towpath, as having 'short golden hair and big padded paws'.

Despite police being inundated with phone calls from terrified witnesses, no lioness showed up. The *Daily Telegraph* of 12 March believed they'd solved the mystery with the headline 'Bilbo the tomcat strikes fear in concrete jungle,' after cat owner Carmel Jarvis came forward to suggest it was her domestic moggie that had been seen.

During June of that year, a puma-like cat was seen by Robert Delane on waste ground near Northolt railway station. He stated that the animal was '3ft tall and 4ft long, with a smooth biscuit-coloured coat.' Robert had been travelling to work on the London Underground when he saw the animal. He told the *Evening Standard*, 'I watched for about two minutes as it walked through the brambles and then it went into some coal bunkers.'

Doug Richardson, a London Zoo expert, stated, 'The description is of a mountain lion. Railway land would suit it perfectly. The animal would be undisturbed and have a plentiful food supply.'

It's no surprise that no lioness or puma turned up, despite a helicopter whirring through the skies of Palmers Green and marksmen from London Zoo lurking in the undergrowth with tranquilliser guns.

Lions are also said to roam the streets of London.

When a ginger tomcat was photographed in a back garden and named as the culprit in the Winchmore sightings, it seemed that the case of the Winchmore Beast had died a quick death. Sightings less frequently littered the pages of the local newspapers, and, although another large cat was sighted at Chiswick in West London in the summer months, evidence was lacking, and the rumours faded.

An African Big Cat in London

Californian student Matt Beloof was only twelve years old when his parents decided to visit England as part of a month-long house swap. One particular evening, as the family were settling into their London home, Matt decided to have a thumb through his London Dungeon pamphlet. Suddenly, he was distracted by a thump from the yard and, looking towards the garden, he was startled to see a huge cat with what he described as 'abnormally illuminated yellowish eyes.'

The animal proceeded to stroll casually across the garden, but with each step had its eye on the shocked witness who gazed from the comforting confines of the living room. The animal then mooched about for a few seconds before disappearing out of sight in the direction of some bushes.

Matt commented, 'London, of all places, is not where you'd expect to see such a thing.'

He described the animal as over 4ft in length and standing 2ft at the shoulder. When Matt told his parents about what he'd seen, they did not believe him.

Such an incident echoed Trevor Irvine's encounter at Hayes Common, Bromley in 1993. He was driving to work at 6.25 a.m. when, just 14ft away, a cat bounded across the road, from the bank on the right-hand side towards the undergrowth on the left. Trevor described the cat as being very large but charcoal grey in colour, with a rosette pattern bleeding through the coat. The cat had small ears on top of a round head, and its tail was very long. After much consideration, he believed he'd seen a black leopard close enough for the rosette pattern to be visible, and the darkness of the coat not as strong.

One evening at 7.45 in January 2001 a woman from Walthamstow observed a sleek, black felid nosing through rubbish bins as she waited in her car to pick her son up. The animal slinked away towards Wickham Close.

The Beast of Bexley

The first reports of the Beast of Bexley emerged from north Kent during the late 1990s, where a creature was dubbed the 'Beast of Bluewater' after numerous reports near the shopping centre. However, regular reports from the outskirts of London, ranging from Bromley, Chislehurst, Penge, Abbey Wood, Belvedere and Crayford, suggested two possibilities: either the local beast was using all these areas as hunting ground, or there was more than one predator. Either way, it would always be dubbed the Beast of Bexley or the Beast of Bluewater in newspaper reports, depending on which area it was closer to when sighted.

On the nights of 20 July and 1 August 2002, Bexley resident Stuart Campbell heard a strange scratching at his back door which awoke him. Concerned about the noises and the safety of his three children, Stuart decided to contact the police and the RSPCA, but his call was not taken seriously.

On 12 July 2003, Nick Allen was staying at the Thistle Tower Hotel, next to Tower Bridge, when he spied a strange cat from his window. The cat, according to Nick, was sculking around the taxi entrance to the hotel from the north end of London Bridge. He described the cat as, 'over large, of russet colour and had a brush on the end of its tail. It had very large and erect ears. I assumed it was an urban fox – but it wasn't – it was feline, far too big, and not canine in its behaviour.'

A year later, residents of Barnehurst, in particular eighteen-year-old Daniel Monck and his sister Tracey, of Cheviot Close, saw a big cat. Daniel's grandmother, eighty-four-year-old Nell Hawes, also saw the cat and feared for her life, refusing to go outside in case the creature was

The surrounding leafy suburbs of London have several 'big cat' legends.

prowling around. Several neighbours reported that a large cat had been seen slinking around the dustbins and feeding off scraps.

On 12 July 2004, an anonymous Bexley resident spotted a large cat at 11 p.m.:

I came out of an alley from Heath Road leading to Cold Blow Crescent and was faced with something sitting next to my car. At first I thought it was a fox, but when I approached it got up to move on and it looked like a big cat. It walked off up my neighbours drive, stopped and turned its head to look at me. When it saw I was still coming (I was walking up my footpath to my front door), it went to the next drive and again turned and stared. I looked at it for a good five minutes without either of us moving.

I've had a quick look on the internet and it looks a bit like a lynx, especially the face, or it was something very similar.

Reports of lynx had been few and far between around the capital, and so it's here that we must rewind three years for our next story …

The Cricklewood Lynx

Since reports began of strange and elusive cats in the countryside, people have always remained a little sceptical to their existence, unless of course they've been fortunate enough to see one. 'Why aren't these animals captured?' seems to be the most common question asked.

Well, in their countries of origin all the cats introduced here thus far are very elusive predators. Leopards, lynx and puma, in the huge territories of their respective countries, are nocturnal hunters which stalk prey with stealth. Apart from those which are hunted, encounters with humans are scarce to the extent that such cats, especially the puma, have taken on a mythical status. Across the United States the animal, which on occasion has been known to attack and kill humans, is known as the 'ghost cat' and 'shadow cat' due to its elusive nature. So, even in the less dense areas of the United Kingdom, where they are alleged to exist, what are the chances of such cats turning up dead on roads, or by the bullet of a hunter? Consider just how rarely foxes and badger carcasses are stumbled upon in the woodlands of the British Isles, and only then can we realise just how slim a chance there is of finding a carcass of a large cat. In 2001, however, an exotic cat was captured.

The *Daily Mail* of 9 May reported, 'LYNX ON THE LOOSE – suburban safari with the Beast of Cricklewood', commenting: 'It was an encounter that no naturalist could ever have imagined … Cricklewood, after all, is the epitome of suburban dullness, where a sudden cry of "Lynx!" would normally signify the last-minute addition of deodorant to the Sainsbury's list.'

The first native to sight the feline visitor to NW2 was letting agent Carol Montague, who mistook the stocky animal with yellowish brown fur and dark spots for a leopard. She was collecting mail from her employer's detached home in Hocroft Lane, when she saw two greenish-grey eyes calmly observing her from a wall outside the kitchen window.

'I could not believe what I was seeing,' said Mrs Montague. 'My first instinct was to think about barricading the house – I've never seen anything like it.'

Mrs Montague contacted the house owners, who in turn telephoned the police who swarmed the place, causing the terrified felid to bolt from the bushes. Attempts to lure the animal into a crate failed. Representatives from London Zoo arrived, but again the cat evaded

Press coverage of the Cricklewood Lynx.

capture. Four hours after the circus began, the cat was finally tranquillised after it attempted to head for the A41. No owner of the animal came forward. The beast was named Lara and was said to have been around eighteen months old and underweight. It was transported to London Zoo and then to a zoo park in France.

Attacked by a Leopard?

We may never get to know the whole truth behind the case of the 'Sydenham Panther', a big, black beast which a resident of south-east London claims attacked him at his home in 2005. What we do know is that the story made headlines across the country. 'Big Cat Attacks Man in Garden,' claimed the BBC website. The *Guardian* were more atmospheric with their 'Fear Stalks the Streets of Sydenham' headline. But what did happen on that fateful morning of 22 March at 2.15?

According to the victim, he had gone into his back garden to look for his pet cat, Kitkat, and was pounced upon by a massive animal, about the size of a labrador. The animal, described as being around 6ft in length, knocked him to the ground and he claimed that he 'was in its claws for about thirty seconds.'

'Its teeth were out and I tried to defend myself and eventually I got the thing off my body.' The *Guardian* website stated that, 'In the gloom … [his] 11-year-old daughter Ashleigh, watched from a bedroom window. 'I just saw my dad flying backwards and struggling with something,' she said. 'I was really scared.'

After the attack, the cat slipped into a neighbour's garden and the man recovered enough to phone the police, who arrived on the scene shortly afterwards. Upon searching the nearby railway line, woods and local allotments, they found no trace of the animal. However, the Metropolitan Police mounted extra patrols and London Zoo officials were consulted.

According to reports, the man was scratched all over his body and suffered bruising to a hand and the back of his head. However, the wounds of the victim were not serious enough to suggest he'd been in the claws of a leopard. Such animals are considered man-eaters in Africa and Asia, so why had this particular animal left no serious markings? Maybe the victim unintentionally exaggerated the attack in his state of shock, or maybe there was no attack at all. This is something we'll never truly get to the bottom of. The police certainly took the matter seriously, and roamed the woods with Taser guns, while local schools were warned of the confrontation.

However, once the attack had happened and police were convinced the animal had left the scene, another big cat mystery was once again left to fade into the annals of folklore.

The Southwark Puma

A Mr Burns claimed that on the morning of 22 April 2008, he'd seen a large felid in the south-east London borough of Southwark.

Mr Burns had been working nights delivering goods, and was in his van in the vicinity of Southwark police station when he spotted an animal he described as 'a cat, about half as large again as a basic domestic cat but with the appearance more like that of a small cougar. I tried to attract its attention but it paid no heed to me whatsoever and walked through the vehicle entrance to the police station.

The witness was adamant he'd seen a cougar. He said the animal appeared tan-coloured, had a long tail and a small head. However, what was such an animal doing in Southwark? After the sighting Mr Burns enquired at the station as to whether they had received any other reports of such an animal but his investigations drew a blank.

The Peckham Rye Pair

During the week commencing 16 March 2008, a Peckham Rye (an area of open space in Southwark) resident contacted the local press to report that he was …

> … just walking my two dogs late this evening when one of them started acting really strangely near the back of the garden area. Then something came out of the shrubs and started to walk

The puma, which is also known as a mountain lion and cougar.

across the path into the picnic area. At first I thought it was a fox, then realised that it was actually bigger than my dog, which is a young Labrador … its tail was long and thin, curling up over its back and it had sandy-coloured fur with a leopard patching. It dawned on me that this was some kind of wild cat … then, seconds later, a second one, smaller, appeared alongside it and they both turned and headed up the path towards the wooded area.

As reports of non-melanistic leopards are scarce across the south, maybe the witness saw a lynx. Of course, until more people come forward to report these 'leopards', such a sighting can only be taken with a pinch of salt.

In August 2009 a family out walking in Norwood, in the wooded area of Church Road and Auckland Road, were alarmed by a 5ft long black cat which approached them. The family fled. The report hit the headlines, with the local press dubbing the creature the 'Palace Puma', despite the fact the animal was black.

In conclusion, judging by the number of eyewitness reports each year pertaining to large cats, it seems that we do indeed have big cats prowling our woods. Some theories put forward by researchers suggest that such animals are in fact not flesh and blood, but possibly demonic, ethereal creatures. This seems unlikely when we consider that many animals have been released or escaped into our wilds to give us the populations we have today. The UK is perfect habitat for these elusive predators, which can survive on a few rabbits a day and shy away from the pursuit of man.

TWO

PHANTOM ASSAILANTS

When Jack the Ripper terrorized the foggy alleyways and courtyards of Victorian London, his crimes would make him world famous. The cloaked predator, who killed five prostitutes around the Whitechapel area in 1888, was never caught and so an air of mystery has forever clouded the case, making the Ripper seem like a prowling phantom. Less harmful, but equally intriguing assailants have littered London lore.

Spring-Heeled Jack

In 1837, fifty-one years before the Ripper's reign of evil, another 'Jack' bounded through the streets of the capital. He became known as Spring-Heeled Jack, and, although his crimes were nowhere near as severe as the Ripper's atrocities, he was another darkly-clad villain who evaded the authorities and invaded the realms of spook lore.

Spring-Heeled Jack, like the Ripper, was never caught. His crimes consisted mainly of assaulting women by way of confronting them, tearing at their garments, revealing their breasts and spouting blue flames into the faces of the stricken victim. The iron-clawed menace seemed to take on supernatural characteristics as he was often described as leaping away at great heights, as if he had springs in his boots, all the while cackling at his dishevelled and torn prey.

In the September of 1837 at Barnes Common (a riverside suburb in the Borough of Richmond-upon-Thames), over the course of two nights, a businessman and three girls were confronted by a laughing spectre with burning eyes. The figure tore at the clothes of the girls and fled into the darkness. The following month, the phantom prowled Cut-Throat Lane, Clapham Common, and groped and attempted to aggressively kiss Mary Stevens as she headed towards Lavendar Hill. Then, the following night, a carriage travelling along Streatham High Road was accosted by a 'creature'. Both coachmen and the footman were injured as the carriage toppled. Shortly after the incident a woman and her two sons observed a tall, thin man who mocked them but did not attack.

On 11 October at Blackheath, south-east London, Polly Adams was assaulted by a mysterious attacker who was described as having glowing eyes, iron-like claws and a mouth that spat blue flame. By late autumn rumours were rife that the beast was stalking Richmond, Kingston and Hampton. In the winter of 1837, two young girls were cornered in Dulwich by the fiend, who ripped the garments from one of the distressed women. It was also alleged that at Forest Gate a couple encountered the darkly-clad ghoul who slashed the face of the man, but the pair were rescued by a gypsy lady who shouted for help.

Spring-Heeled Jack's crimes were often considered those of a strange and sadistic prankster, and the vicious acts were addressed on 9 January 1838 by the Lord Mayor at Mansion House, in which he called the midnight marauder a 'ghost', 'bear' and 'devil'.

Meanwhile, in the same month, a villain known as the Peckham Ghost was stalking the streets and had allegedly attacked and even killed in areas of Vauxhall, Brixton and Stockwell. In St John's Wood the monster attacked for two weeks, and police predicted that six murders would occur. They never did.

The name Spring-Heeled Jack was born in the late January of 1838 and the following month, sisters Lucy and Margaret Scales, while visiting their brother Tom at Narrow Street, Limehouse, had a frightful meeting with the brute. It was 8.35 p.m. when the women left Tom's home, and, as they strode along a dimly lit passageway, Lucy saw a fleeting figure which then pounced. She was enveloped in his cloak, the figure held a lantern which illuminated his mouth of blue flame, and then the apparition was gone. Two days later, at the home of a Mr Alsop, a knock at the door at a late hour disturbed the three Alsop sisters, Mary (sixteen), Jane (eighteen) and the married Sarah. Jane went to the door and in the gloom saw a tall, dark figure wearing a top hat, who bellowed, 'I am a policeman, for God's sake bring me a light we have caught Spring-Heeled Jack here in the lane!'

With that, Jane went to fetch a candle, but, upon turning around, she was met by the figure which Londoners had become so fearful of. With eyes apparently aglow and mouth aflame, Jack slashed at Jane's clothes, but her sister Sarah came running to the rescue and took on the helmeted spectre, who set off into the night.

Many more alleged attacks would occur concerning the so-called leaping phantom. In every case, leading up until 1845, similar details were described: the shining eyes, the glinting claws which so easily cut through garments, that mouth of flame, the hideous mocking laughter, and the way the apparition fled into the darkness, bounding like he had springs in his shoes.

Reports after 1845 are somewhat vague but have been recorded. The spindly man was allegedly seen at Dulwich College, south-east London, and was also said to have attacked a wagon at Lordship Lane. There are even some twentieth-century reports of the monster and

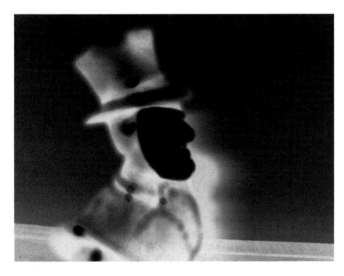

Spring-Heeled Jack – the darkly-clad phantom assailant of old London.

those from further north at Aldershot and Merseyside, but, despite exhaustive research, no one has ever solved the riddle. The finger of blame did once point to the rather eccentric Marquis of Waterford, a local prankster and Irish nobleman who had a hatred for women, but when he died, in 1859, the attacks continued further north in Norfolk in 1877 (although it is possible that these were copycat assaults).

Just like the mystery of Jack the Ripper, the attacks from Spring-Heeled Jack provoked much response and theory over the years, with some people believing that the slasher was in fact an extraterrestrial or vicious ghost. The facts of the crimes remain murky as, over time, an air of folklore has enshrouded the spate of attacks. It seems that, despite the savagery and clandestine behaviour that Spring-Heeled Jack bestowed upon the capital, his crimes may well have been overly exaggerated in local press stories, especially when we look back at such publications as the *Illustrated Police News*, which in the 1800s were quick to dramatise accounts of such encounters.

The Hammersmith Ghost

A few decades prior to Spring-Heeled Jack, in 1804, the 'Hammersmith Ghost' prowled. This white-cloaked figure was said to haunt the alleyways of the London Borough of Hammersmith and Fulham, frightening the life out of hapless victims. On one occasion the 'ghost' literally did frighten the life out of a heavily pregnant woman, who was so startled that she died within two days of the incident. The spectre even attacked a wagon rumbling through the streets, pulled by eight horses.

Old records state that the 'ghost' was simply a local man, possibly a shoemaker, who carried out the attacks. When in custody, the man claimed he did it out of revenge as his own children had been scared by his apprentices and their ghost stories.

However, twenty years later, a far more vicious set of assaults would take place in Hammersmith, pre-dating the malicious Spring-Heeled attacks by over a decade – or was it the same individual? Several women had been accosted by a figure who scratched them and

Did a ghost haunt
Hammersmith in 1804?

Hammersmith.

caused several victims to have fits. Some of the women claimed that they'd been scratched by a hook-like object. The vile prowler was certainly keen to make a name for himself for he daubed many doors and gates across town with strange writings in chalk. 'Be ye ready', stated one piece of graffiti, another, 'Prepare to die!' and a third, 'Your end is near.'

Men were asked to guard some of the areas that had experienced high levels of activity, and then, after eight-weeks, the predator was caught. They said he was simply a respectable young man named John Benjamin, a farmer from Harrow.

And yet, eight years later, on the fringe of the Spring-Heeled Jack attacks, another Hammersmith sociopath began a reign of terror. This time the figure was adorned in a white cloak or dress, had long claws and was able to scale high walls with ease. Other reports, which would bear a striking resemblance to Spring-Heeled Jack, suggested an armoured spectre.

One eerie fact seems to connect many of London's phantom assailants: it was reported by the local press, including the *West London Observer*, that the Hammersmith Ghost was an assailant that appears every fifty years, and indeed the older case of the London Monster (mentioned later in this chapter), Spring-Heeled Jack, and then Jack the Ripper, all fit into this fifty-year cycle. And of course, none of these assailants were ever caught …

A Horned Figure

Two centuries before the Hammersmith Ghost, a frightful humanoid was said to prowl the meat markets of East London. The 1654 journal *Mercurious Democritus* recorded that every Saturday night this spectre would terrorise the areas of Whitechapel and Eastcheap, spooking the tradesmen by pushing their goods to the floor from their stalls. Those who became infuriated by the apparition hacked and slashed at it, only to see their weapons of choice pass through its body without effect. The figure was often described as being horned and wearing shoes or having feet with long, curled ends. Some who feared the tormentor claimed it was the spirit of a man named Mallet who had been a local lawyer. No one knows why the

A horned, devilish figure roamed areas such as Eastcheap.

Lombard Street in the City.

creature haunted the area and chose the market stalls to fulfil its wrath, but in his 1964 book *The Realm of Ghosts*, Eric Maple theorises that maybe 'he had died from food poisoning' from meat purchased from a stall!

This monster echoed a critter from 1647 at Lombard Street in the City of London. The phantom was said to roam the yard of a Mr Youngs and appeared as a prankster spirit which 'reduced learned men to fits of ecstasy so that they could not speak or stand'. In his book *Ghosts of London*, J.A. Brooks transcribed:

> ... this hideous monster ... usually vanishes away (to the thinking of the beholders) into the ground, then immediately ensueth a noise like to claps of thunder and flashes of fire like lightning seemes to ascend out of the Earthe, and after that a stinking mist, and a noisome sulferous smoake.

Four decades later, an assailant known as Whipping Tom was said to prowl the shadows of Chancery Lane, Fleet Street, Strand, Holborn and Fetter Lane. His bizarre attacks centred upon women who were accosted, their dresses lifted and their buttocks spanked with a metal rod as the attacker shouted, 'Spanko!'

Such was the swiftness of the predator that many believed this perverse character possessed supernatural ability. The phantom was never caught but inspired a book entitled *Whipping Tom Brought to Light and Exposed to View*.

The London Monster

Between 1788 and 1790 (100 years before the Ripper, and fifty years prior to Spring-Heeled Jack) the London Monster caused chaos in the capital. This vicious jester had a repertoire of sadism including stabbing women in the face through a fake nosegay, slashing at clothing and then running off into the night, hurling obscenities in his wake. In certain attacks he even attached razorblades to his knees and stabbed women's buttocks in a vile frenzy, leaving more than fifty victims with shredded clothing and sliced flesh. Unfortunately, descriptions of the beast were too inconsistent, and, with local panic hitting the streets, a NO MONSTER CLUB was formed, allowing men to wear badges in order to let terrified women know that they were not the monster and indeed approachable. Even the famed Bow Street Runners could not capture the jabber, and local thieves had a field-day amongst the piquerism and panic.

Finally, after an encounter at St James Park, twenty-three-year-old Rhynwick Williams was accused of the crimes after he was seen following Anne Porter. Despite having an alibi for all the other attacks, Williams was made a scapegoat to ease the pressure and was charged by the magistrates for the defacement of clothing – which at the time was given a harsher penalty than attempted murder! After an absurd hearing Rhynwick was given a retrial, but, despite the shoddy evidence against him, he was handed a six-year jail term. The attacks did continue, but sporadically, and the London Monster faded into folklore, just like the assailants who would follow him.

The Vampire of the West End

On 16 April 1912 at 6 a.m., a local clerk was walking to work, heading down Coventry Street, in London's West End, when he was suddenly accosted from the shadows by an unseen form which stabbed him in the throat. The man collapsed to the floor unconscious and later woke in Charing Cross Hospital. He told surgeons of his ordeal but would not divulge anything about himself. The doctors believed he was simply attacked by someone lying in wait. However, two hours later, another man was admitted to the hospital with identical wounds and a matching story, from the exact same location, and once again he would say nothing about himself! Later that evening a third attack took place at Coventry Street, and yes, *déjà-vu*.

The police could not fathom what had happened and were bewildered by the coincidences. The press were quick to lap up the events of the day, with the *Daily Mail* reporting that the sinister predator may well be a vampire.

No vampire, or human culprit, was ever apprehended.

Hair Clippers and Skirt Snippers

In 1911, after several reported attacks in Middlesex and Kent, an Enfield resident, who was a typist at a London Constitutional Club, was approaching the clubhouse one morning when she was grabbed by an unknown assailant and her hair cut. Two other similar incidents took place, but on the third occasion the perpetrator was caught and arraigned at Mansion House.

In most cases where victims, usually women, fall foul to this such vicious and weird predation, the hair is very rarely found, suggesting that some kinky snipper likes to collect the hairy trophies.

Did a vampire lurk in the evening shadows of Coventry Street around 1912?

The Phantom Skirt-Slasher of Piccadilly held reign for six-months during the 1960s, a teasing menace who loitered behind women on escalators and cut fabric from their skirts to reveal their buttocks. In 1977 the pest, or possibly a similar person, struck again, and became known as Jack the Snipper. He would flee into the depths of London Underground after his attacks. The skirt-ripper never wounded his victims, in fact most were unaware they'd even been a victim. In 1977 the phantom was caught, and turned out to be twenty-three-year-old school career officer Graham Carter, who'd even kept a diary of his exploits. He was ordered to pay £270 for his crimes.

The Platform Maniac

The Platform Maniac was a murderous entity said to have haunted the London Underground during the 1980s. Author Michael Goss discussed the phantom killer in 1985, in issue 19 of the *Magonia* magazine (pages 3-6). He stated that such was the potency of the legend that it drew comparisons with the rumours on the other side of the world that alligators were inhabiting the sewer systems beneath New York. Of course, while there may have been one or two incidents where unwanted pets had been flushed down the toilet, the Platform Maniac was a different ball game altogether. Here was a fiend said to lurk on crowded platforms, and, with a simple nudge, push people in front of approaching trains, before slinking off into the background. The killer was also said to roam the more desolate stations, seeking out victims.

In 2004 a patient on day release from North London's St Luke's Hospital attempted to push a woman onto tracks of the London Underground system. Such incidents, along with the occasional tragic accident or suicide on the tracks, fuelled the rumours. However, in reality there was no Platform Maniac, just excited whispers and local mania.

A similar urban legend arose in the 1980s and '90s when night-clubbers throughout London and the south-east were said to dance in fear of an elusive predator who would prowl the dark

During the 1980s the platforms of the London Underground were said to be prowled by a murderous maniac.

dance floors with syringe in hand, injecting HIV into chosen victims. When the victims got home they would find a note in their pocket which read, 'Welcome to AIDS Club'. Chilling stuff, but true?

The Phantom Cat-Ripper

On 5 September 1998 the 'This is Local London' website reported on a grisly find:

A dead cat, with its head cut off, is the latest gruesome find in a series of bizarre attacks on animals across London. The cat was found with its head missing and most of its blood drained, in Main Road, Sidcup, last Thursday. It was removed by Bexley Council environmental health officers. Several months ago another cat was found in a front garden of a house in Penshurst Avenue, Sidcup. Its head and tail had been removed. There was also a similar incident in Erith.

A total of forty suspicious deaths among pets have taken place in the last ten months and the most common victims are domestic cats.

RSPCA inspector Nigel Shelton said, 'The number of cases of animals which have been decapitated or had limbs removed from their bodies is growing at an alarming rate and we would urge anybody with any information to contact us urgently.'

A month later a sixty-eight-year-old Wimbledon resident was traumatised after neighbours found the head of her pet cat in their garden at Caxton Road. In November of that year it seemed as though the cat-ripper was on the move. Cats and rabbits had been found either decapitated or stripped of flesh at Tottenham, Stepney, and New Barnet. A psychiatrist was called in to attempt to assemble a profile of the killer.

On 19 December the killer struck again. Bonkers, a cat belonging to Eileen Tattershall from Twickenham, was found by a neighbour. The victim's head and tail had been removed. However, an RSPCA inspector investigating the rippings concluded that the deaths could be blamed on vehicles, despite the fact that many cats had been found in woods or back gardens, and not in the close proximity of a road.

Was the phantom cat-ripper an elusive 'big cat'?

Despite the initial spate of slayings, the killings gradually subsided, but occurred sporadically until 2004. Some believed a pet serial killer was on the loose, others blamed a large cat such as a puma, a beast also known as the 'M25 Monster', but no one knows for sure who, or what the cat-ripper was.

Less Threatening Tormentors

In 1924 London tram-driver John Pitman was arrested for slipper-snatching! After being caught in the act all he had to say was, 'I don't know why I did it. I am very sorry. I am married.'

In 1977 Metropolitan newspaper the *Job*, and also the *Sun* and *Daily Mirror*, reported on 'the phantom wall-smasher' after a spate of unusual acts of vandalism mainly in the Peckham area. Between July and September of that year, an unseen 'wall-banger' went on the rampage on Danby Street. Entire walls would be found by house owners in piles in their gardens or smashed or toppled, but no sign of the individual responsible. Some residents believed there must have been some deranged person, who, for some unknown reason, was angry with the rest of the street, but no one could pinpoint why exactly this vandalism was being carried out.

Children were ruled out of the attacks because some of the damage had to have been caused by a robust figure – maybe it was a local builder or ex-bricklayer who had become unhinged through unemployment, and decided to take his frustration out on the walls he'd built!

Victims of the mystery yob had to pay out hundreds and thousands of pounds for repair work. The first alleged victim claimed they'd been in their garden when it happened. They had popped indoors to fetch a milk bottle but upon returning seconds later were shocked to see the garden full of rubble and no front wall! There had been no sound to report either. Two other residents didn't do a very good job at keeping watch over each other's property; both nipped to the toilet and returned to see their walls reduced to a pile of bricks.

Only in one case of many was a sound reported (that being two thumps) and in no case was a person seen fleeing the scene and no tools were ever found at the scenes. However, as the colder months drew in the damage ceased. If some peculiar individual was to blame, it's clear they were a wall short of a brick or two!

THREE

THE HIGHGATE VAMPIRE

Welcome to the world of the dead – and the world of the undead: Highgate Cemetery. Highgate Cemetery is situated in North London, its overgrown grounds are punctured by monolithic symbols of the past and web-ridden catacombs embrace the dead. It is divided into eastern and western segments (which are dissected by the serpentile of Swains Lane, constructed 1830), and both burial grounds are only a ten-minute stride from the reputedly haunted Highgate station, where a phantom train is said to rumble.

The East Cemetery, the resting place of philosopher Karl Marx (1818-1883), is overgrown at its heart, but it is more open to the cold air than its shadowed relation across the road and is, in general, far more 'arranged' than its neighbour. In fact, the eastern section is almost like any other graveyard. However, it does claim to have a ghost; a phantom female said to wander among the crooked tombs looking for the children she allegedly murdered.

The West Cemetery is one of Gothic splendour, bordered by thick, robust perimeter platforms which, in Victorian times, allowed the public to view the cemetery and its funerals. In its early days the cemetery was actually a burial place for plague victims. However, during the Victorian era its grim confines were turned into one of prestige, where the rich and famous were buried, their cadavers given the devotion of one mighty crypt or leering white pillar. It became a grand gravesite, where, for three guineas (a fee far beyond the reach of average members of the public at the time), one could guarantee an admirable resting place.

During the latter half of the twentieth century the cemetery fell into disrepair, but it has since been restored to something of its former glory by The Friends of Highgate Cemetery and today the cemetery has a tranquil air. However, during the 1960s, when the cemetery was a semi-derelict and thorny labyrinth, terrifying rumours of a phantom creature began to sweep the area. The spectre, which become known worldwide as the Highgate Vampire, was said to be a black, 7ft tall, red-eyed ghoul reported to haunt the Swains Lane area and also the north gate of the West Cemetery, which is no longer in use.

Investigations at the time, and many headlines in the local *Hampstead & Highgate Express*, painted a picture of a blood-drinking apparition, rumoured to have visited the homes of several women residing nearby and left puncture marks on their necks.

Then, in late 1969, a witness of the Highgate Vampire claimed that something had hypnotised him while he was looking for his way out of the overgrown cemetery after becoming lost. The man had been seeking out the gate when he became aware of a tall figure very close by, a strange, dark presence that seemed to be draining him of life. The man claimed that the figure was floating slightly off the ground and it seemed to transfix him with terror. A couple of other

Highgate Cemetery.

The less foreboding East Cemetery.

Swains Lane separates the eastern and western burial ground.

witnesses came forward; one was a woman who claimed that while walking her dog near the cemetery she became aware of a dark form hovering behind the gates. The figure began to screech and howl, and then it vanished into thin air. At the time, several foxes were also found dead in the cemetery, but there were no signs as to how the creatures died.

On the evening of 21 December 1969, local paranormal researcher David Farrant decided to spend the night in the cemetery, in the hope of spotting the phantom.

David walked down Swains Lane at around 11 p.m. and in one particular area he felt an overwhelming presence, as though he was not alone. He approached the gate with the intention of scaling it, but when he peered into the darkness he noticed something moving in the distance. Maybe his eyes were playing tricks in the gloom; maybe shadows cast by the tombstones and bracken were creating demons that were not really there. Yet something appeared to be moving a few metres away. Then, just five yards inside the gate, he saw it: a large, black shape. He tried to dismiss it as merely a fellow trespasser inside the grounds, but no. It was over 7ft tall and had two red eyes which met his gaze; it was not a human presence, but some astral thing attempting to drain him under some kind of hypnotic state. Then, quite suddenly, the figure vanished.

In his book, *Beyond the Highgate Vampire*, Farrant states:

> … stories of an apparition at Highgate Cemetery had by no means begun with the current sightings. Indeed, similar tales dated back to the Victorian era and, interestingly enough, many of them had 'vampiristic' connotations.
>
> Perhaps the reason for this was that Bram Stoker himself had been influenced by the existence of 'something' in Highgate Cemetery. When he wrote *Dracula* in 1897, he made direct reference to Highgate Cemetery (or at least an area in the close vicinity) as being the last resting place of one of Count Dracula's disciples. Stoker may also have been influenced by the eerie case of Elizabeth Siddal, who died in 1855 and was buried in Highgate Cemetery. In 1862 her body was exhumed by a relative anxious to retrieve some poems said to have been in her coffin, and a witness called Charles Augustas Howell described the 'awesome sight' of the undecayed body with ' luxuriant red-gold hair' that, 'practically filled the coffin' – the implication being that Elizabeth Siddal was 'undead', or in a state of catalepsy.

Indeed, many cases of victims rising from death emerged during the Victorian era, with people allegedly having been buried in a comatose state instead of actually being dead. It is said that many 'corpses' were accompanied by bells when buried, just in case they woke and needed to alert the guard. Did such tales create the legends of figures moaning and scratching at their coffin lid, and at times rising?

In February 1970 several letters from witnesses to the local ghoul began to appear in the local *Hampstead & Highgate Express*, under the heading of 'The Ghost of N6':

> With reference to the letter in last week's *Ham & High*, many local people have seen Mr Farrant's ghost in Highgate Cemetery. The ghost will sometimes appear nightly for about a week and then not be seen again for perhaps a month. To my knowledge the ghost always takes the form of a pale figure and has been appearing for several years.
>
> K. FREWIN, N6

The North Gate of
the West Cemetery –
and regular haunt of
the 'vampire'.

My fiancée and I spotted a most unusual form about a year ago; it just seemed to glide across the path. Although we waited a little while it did not reappear again. I am glad somebody else has spotted it; I was convinced it was not my imagination.

AUDREY CONNELY, N6

There is without doubt a ghost. Of when and whom he originated I do not know. Many tales are told, however, about a tall man in a hat who walks across Swains Lane and just disappears through a wall in the cemetery. Local superstition also has it that the bells in the old disused chapel toll mysteriously whenever he walks.

R. DOCHERTY

Something was indeed stirring within the ivy-strewn alleyways of Highgate. Suddenly, television crews, hoaxers, reporters and amateur researchers converged upon the area. Some investigators were prosecuted for all manner of alleged crimes from trespassing to occult activities. In 1970 the *Hampstead & Highgate Express* reported, 'Does a Wampyr Walk in Highgate?':

'We don't want to frighten you, but the ghost of Highgate Cemetery might be a vampire.' So says Sean Manchester, president of the British Occult Society. He claims to have carried out 'extensive research and investigation into the matter'. Mr Manchester, a twenty-five-year-old photographer, said, 'The phenomenon reported by Highgate people in letters to the *Ham & High* is not merely the apparition of an earth-bound spirit, which is relatively harmless, but much worse – that of a wampyr, or as it is more popularly known, a vampire.'

His theory is that the King Vampire of the Undead, originally a nobleman who dabbled in black magic in medieval Wallachia, 'somewhere near Turkey', walks again.

'His followers eventually brought him to England in a coffin at the beginning of the eighteenth century and bought a house for him in the West End,' said Mr Manchester. 'His

The path frequently prowled by a tall, dark figure.

unholy resting place is Highgate Cemetery. When parts of Britain were plagued by vampirism centuries ago, the Highgate area was the centre of a lot of activity; it has been ever since. And now there is so much desecration of graves by Satanism, I'm convinced that this has been happening in Highgate Cemetery in an attempt by a body of Satanists to resurrect the King Vampire.'

More letters to the newspaper certainly suggested a malevolent figure: J. McKennar of N10 wrote:

A frightening experience occurred on the Heath. I was passing beside the viaduct pond when a figure on the far side beckoned me. As I approached, the figure started wading in the water, staring at me with a horrific look. It continued into the pond, motioning me to follow.

I knew that what I was looking at was not human, as there were no ripples in the water around it. With a terrible cry the head disappeared beneath the still water, leaving me trembling.

Towards the end of April 1970, a young woman claimed she had been thrown to the ground by a tall, black figure as she walked past the cemetery one night. The thing had a deathly white face, yet it disappeared when a motorist pulled up to help her.

David Farrant decided a séance should be performed in the cemetery to try to identify the apparition and its origin and purpose, if it had one. The date for this gathering was to be 17 August 1970. According to Sean Manchester and the *Hampstead & Highgate Express*, such an 'exorcism' had already been conducted after several bouts of grave vandalism, and was mentioned on 7 August 1970 under the heading, 'That Vampire Back Again?', which stated that 'Convinced that the desecration was part of a secret Satanic meeting, Mr Manchester has since exorcised the vault with an occult ceremony using crucifixes, holy water and garlic.'

Numerous arrests, alleged satanic activity and further investigations into the vampire followed, and the following autumn a man was found dying in the cemetery. He was drenched with blood and had been stabbed in the chest and throat, but it was concluded that his wounds were self-inflicted.

On 1 October 1971 the local paper featured a report under the heading 'Nicked by the Ghost Squad':

Two young men decided to spend the night in Highgate Cemetery '… for the experience'. They armed themselves with a crucifix and a sharpened wooden stake in case they met a vampire. As they crept around the tombs at midnight three burly figures suddenly sprang up from behind gravestones. The trio were policemen – members of the 'ghost squad' set up to combat black magic devotees believed to be responsible for the desecration at the cemetery.

The two men were arrested and appeared at Clerkenwell this week. Simon Wiles, 18 and James White, 20, were both cleared of conspiring to cause damage to coffins and tombs. When questioned Mr White said, 'We were just going to stay the night. Legend has it that if one meets the vampire one drives a stake through its heart.'

Three decades later it appears as though the fuss surrounding the so-called vampire has died down. However, in the summer of 2006 a man walking down Swains Lane saw a dark figure standing near the gates of the West Cemetery. Upon approaching, the man noticed that the figure was dressed in a long, dark coat and had a tall, black hat perched on its head. In a strange, old-fashioned accent the figure said, 'Good evening sir' and, despite being some distance away, the witness claimed that the voice was right in his ear. When the man walked by the figure and looked back, he was astonished to see the being floating across the road and through the gates of the eastern entrance.

In 2007 a female motorist travelling along Swains Lane saw a tall, dark figure with glowing yellow eyes which walked through a wall. Then, just days later, a witness walking their dog

Highgate is said to sit on a mystical ley-line which runs through The Gatehouse pub, Highgate Wood, and The Flask pub, as well as the cemetery. All of these locations have been haunted by a dark figure.

in Highgate Woods had an alleged confrontation with a dark spectre which vanished into thin air.

The legend of the 'vampire' of Highgate has been clouded in mystery for the last thirty years, mainly due to the local hysteria it created, but whatever lurked in the cemetery is possibly still there, lying dormant until triggered by human intervention. The Highgate Vampire will always be one of London's most intriguing cases.

Some have dismissed the sightings as being nothing more than extras from Hammer horror films being made at the time. However, researcher Alan Friswell discovered that only one vampire film was actually made in Highgate Cemetery, this being *The Body Beneath*, directed by Andy Milligan, but the film involved hippies and not cloaked creatures. The alleged Hammer films responsible for the so-called vampire apparition had in fact been made two years previously; *Taste the Blood of Dracula*, starring Christopher Lee being the most famous. Amicus Films used some of the tombstones and ivy-strewn pathways in 1972 and '73, for the title sequences of films such as *Tales from the Crypt* and *Beyond the Grave*.

Finally, there are two other reports from the 1960s which have rarely seen the light of day with regard to the vampire craze. Firstly, David Farrant recorded a sighting from 1965 when a male witness saw a black ooze slide from the cemetery and transform into a figure. However, the most bizarre sighting took place around 1967/68 and was mentioned in the first issue of *Suspended In Dusk*, a magazine put together by Mr Farrant and several friends. The report, submitted by a man named Johnny, read:

It was a dark, clear night and I walked down Swains Lane. When I got to about the place where the broken wall is, I saw an old lady ahead of me. The lady turned into a large leopard or giant black cat with red eyes. A car approached, the cat snarled, shot across the road toward the cemetery and over the wall. It was clearly outlined in the headlights. The driver must have seen it. It was very large and, after that, I was not keen to venture down Swains Lane.

FOUR

ANIMAL APPARITIONS

SPECTRAL DOGS

All over Britain and across the world come legends of fiery-eyed hellhounds, the most popular being Black Shuck (said to haunt the Norfolk, Suffolk and Essex coastline), Padfoot (from Yorkshire and Staffordshire), Stryker (Lancashire and Yorkshire) and Guytrash (West Yorkshire), all of which are considered bad omens. Some of these spectral accomplices walk by the side of weary travellers, and, at times, lead them astray.

The Phantom Hound of Newgate Prison

The old Newgate Prison once sat at the corner of Newgate Street and Old Bailey, inside the City of London. It harbours one of the capital's most terrifying apparitions, that of an evil black hound. The legend of the dog dates back to the reign of Henry III and the most fascinating account originates from the pen of Luke Hutton, who was an inmate in the 1500s and was hanged at the prison in 1598. An oft-repeated version comes from 1638, entitled *The Discovery of a London Monster*, and reads as follows:

> I maintained that I had read an old Chronicle that it was a walking spirit in the likeness of a blacke Dog, gliding up and down the streets a little before the time of Execution, and in the night while Sessions continued, and his beginning thus.
>
> In the raigne of King Henry the third there happened such a famine through England, but especially in London, that many starved for want of food, by which meanes the Prisioners

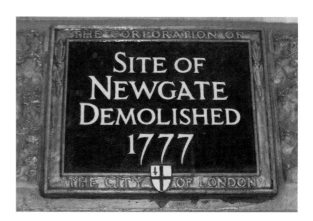

The site of Newgate Prison.

A malevolent hellhound once haunted Newgate Prison.

in Newgate eat up one another altue, but commonly those that came newly in … there was a certain scholar brought tither, upon suspicion of Conjuring, and that he by Charmes and devilish Whitchcrafts, had done much hurt to the kings subjects, which Scholler, mauger his Devil Furies, Spirits and Goblins, was by the famished prisoners eaten up …

With vengeance promised by the prey: … nightly to see the Scholler in the shape of a black Dog walking up and downe the Prison, ready with ravening Jawes to teare out their bowles; for his late human flesh they had so hungerly eaten, and withal they hourely heard (as they thought) strange groanes and cries, as if it had been some creature in great paine and torments, whereupin such a nightly feare grew amongst them, that it turned into a Frenzie, and from a Frenzie to Desperation, in which desperation they killed the keeper, and so many of them escaped forth, but yet whither soever they came or went they imagined a Blacke Dog to follow, and by this means, as I doe thinke, the name of him began.

The Wandsworth Road Apparition

Another, less frightening, hound was said to materialize at No. 523 Wandsworth Road during the 1960s. A proprietor of a fish restaurant wrote a letter to the Society for Psychical Research in December 1962:

I respectfully bring to your notice a phenomena that has occurred at the above address, and trust that it may be of sufficient interest for your investigation, which I would welcome.

In the April of this year, I opened a Fish restaurant here. The business potential was very good, and the weekly turnover increased rapidly over the first four months.

In the last six or seven weeks of that period, a large black and beautiful dog was seen to pass from the rear rooms of the premises through the shop, and out into the street, from whence it would turn right, and lope away up the main road and out of sight. This 'visitation' occurred six or seven times, always between 6 and 6.30 p.m., and when we were sitting at a table, in the then empty shop, and with the rear door locked. On one occasion he brushed solidly against my wife's leg, and on each appearance was seen by three of us clearly.

Strangely, when the sightings stopped, the takings of the shop seemed to plummet. However, shortly afterwards, an explanation was offered as to whose dog had been haunting the premises. It seems that a black dog was owned by a previous proprietor until it was run over and killed at a near by cross-roads.

A dog resembling a dachshund is said to haunt an area of Baker Street. Similar harmless ghost dogs have been seen along the Thames. Phantom dogs are said to also prowl a stairwell at Hampton Court, the Anchor Tavern on Bankside and the Spanish Galleon pub in Greenwich, which is apparently haunted by a large mastiff hound. Again, these are thought to be the spirits of deceased pets.

The Beast of St Michael's

The 'beast' which visited St Michael's, a medieval parish church in the City of London, was far from a ghostly pet.

The Tudor historian John Stow (1525-1605) recorded a strange story told to him by his father:

> My father told me that, at St Michael's church in the Cornhill ward, London, on the night of St James, certain men were ringing the bells of St Michael's, in the loft, when there arose a tempest of thunder and lightning, and a thing of an ugly shape and sight was seen to come in at the south window, and it lighted on the north. For fear whereof, all the ringers fell down and lay as dead for a time, leaving the bells to ring and cease of their own accord. When the ringers came to themselves, they found certain stones of the north window to be razed and scrat as if they had been so much butter, printed with a lion's claw; the same stones were fastened there again, when it was repaired, and remain so to this day. I have seen them oft, and have put a feather or small stick into the hole where the claw had entered, three to four inches deep.

St Michael's Church.

At the same time, certain main Timber posts at Queen Hith were scrat and cleft from top to bottom, and the Pulpit Cross in Paul's churchyard was likewise scrat, cleft and overturned. One of the ringers lived in my youth, whom I have oft heard to verifye the same to be true, and I have oft heard my Father to report it.

The Spectral Dog of Soho

Paranormal author Elliot O'Donnell was a master at collating mysterious tales. In his *Casebook of Ghosts* he mentions several phantom dogs said to have haunted the capital. One of the most intriguing of these ghosts involved a friend of the author who encountered an apparition at the old Motley Club, which was located in Dean Street, Soho.

Just before the club shut down, the witness, a man named Dickson, was at the premises when he observed a yellow dog of some size, which confronted him on a staircase. Dickson, hoping to provoke no ferocity from the strange dog, threw it a biscuit, but the dog did not bat an eyelid at the nibble. It then slowly padded past Dickson and out of sight. The next day Dickson once again frequented the stairwell, and was shocked once again to meet the yellow hound. Again, the man threw it a biscuit. Again, the cookie was ignored, and again the dog passed him. This time, however, Dickson kept his eyes trained on the animal, and was startled to see it vanish into thin air halfway down the stairs. On the third visit, Dickson once again observed the creature, but this time he threw it a piece of meat, and once again the animal took no notice. Baffled by the dog, Dickson decided to prod the animal with his stick, but was amazed to see the cane pass through the animal, which then faded from view. Dickson was clearly fed up with the surreal *déjà-vu* and visited the club no more, but he was told of other witnesses who'd seen the spectral dog until the club shut down.

GHOSTLY CATS

Tales of deceased pets are common-place in ghost lore, but the following accounts are more unusual when it comes to yarns of the felid kind.

The Legless Felid

One of the most obscure cases of a spectral cat emerges from a 1674 pamphlet discovered in the Guildhall Library. The house in which the following was observed seemed to have a reputation for all manner of spooky goings on.

The pamphlet was entitled *News from Puddle-Dock in London Or, A Perfect particular of the strange Apparitions and Transactions that have happened in the House of Mr Edward Pitts next Door to the Still at Puddle-dock*:

> … Mr Pitts takes the Loaf off the Dresser to cut bread to lay on the Table, as he was cutting the Bread he spied upon the Dresser a great thing like a Catt, at which being a little affrighted, he started back Presently calling to his Wife, saying, here's a Catt, I never saw a Catt in this house before, upon which, this Cat-like thing seemed to slide off the Dresser, giving a thump on the Boards, and so vanished away. All Mr Pitt's Family then in the Room, but none could perceive

this strange Catt but only his daughter of about 15 years of Age, and himself; and they say it was as bigg as any Mastiff Dog; but they could not perceive that it had any Leggs.

Cats around the Capital

During the 1950s in east London at 88 Newark Street, there was said to lurk a ghostly cat. It terrorised the occupants on occasion and was usually seen by the children of the house. The family believed they were cursed by the creature, which they felt had bestowed upon them six years of ill luck.

A decade previously, a spectral cat was said to haunt Great Tower Street in the City. The phantom was often seen prowling around the church before the building was destroyed by German bombers in the Second World War. The most bizarre sighting of the creature involved a handful of witnesses who claimed to have seen a ghostly woman who transformed into the cat and slinked away.

During the 1930s at Regent's Park Zoo, a keeper taking leave was strolling through the grounds with his granddaughter one afternoon when a lion with a glowing coat sauntered by. Thinking one of the beasts had escaped its cage, the keeper went to raise the alarm, but not before the cat suddenly vanished into thin air. The next morning, upon returning to work, the keeper found that one of the lions had died at exactly the same time the apparition appeared.

In 1992 a large, yellow-coloured cat was seen in the vicinity of West End Lane, in the Borough of Camden. Several witnesses were spooked by the apparition, which they described as having an eerie hue about it.

In the 1970s at a house in Thornton Heath, a Mrs Forbes claimed to have been the victim of violent poltergeist activity. This included household objects being thrown about the place by an invisible force and attacks committed by a vampire-like apparition. On another occasion Mrs Forbes claimed that a cat resembling a spectral tiger had scratched and clawed her.

A large, ghostly Persian specimen is said to be sighted at All Hallows by the Tower, which is the oldest church in the City. Legend has it that the church organist who died, left a message stating that she wished her domestic cat be buried on consecrated ground once its time was up. However, it is believed that the vicar at the time did not carry out the wish and so the cat is said to forever lurk around the church.

There should be a ghostly cat of Stanmore when you consider that one afternoon in the January of 1987, local moggie Peppi went for a stroll around Anmer Lodge and suddenly exploded in a flash of blue flame!

The Phantom Roar

Mrs Laursen reported to the website 'Spicy Cauldron' that her London home (location unknown) had been haunted by a disembodied roar. The phantom growl often emanated from the passageway of the flat which she shared with her husband, and always when she was about to feed her six domestic cats. The eerie snarl occurred for more than a year, despite having no discernible source. There was never any sign of a spectral lion although a theory was put forward, with tongue firmly in cheek, that maybe a spirit cat from London Zoo had prowled out of its ghostly territory.

The couple eventually grew out of the flat and waved goodbye to the phantom roar.

PHANTOM BIRDS

The Horror of West Drayton Church

There could be all manner of ghostly animals lurking in our countryside, but would we really know if we've seen one? The following case, as documented by Revd F.G. Lee in his *Glimpses in the Twilight* (1885), remains one of London's most intriguing stories, and pertains to a spectral flapper.

Lee wrote:

In the middle of the last century, circa 1749, owing to several remarkable circumstances which had then recently occurred, a conviction became almost universal among the inhabitants of the village, that the vaults under the church of West Drayton, near Uxbridge, were haunted. Strange noises were heard in and about the sacred building, and the sexton of that day, a person utterly devoid of superstition, was on inquiry and examination compelled to admit that certain unaccountable occurrences in regard to the vault had taken place ... Others maintained that three persons from an adjacent mansion-house in company had gone to look through a grating in the side of the foundation of the church – for the ventilation of the vault, and from which screams and noises were heard constantly, and had there seen a very large black raven perched on one of the coffins. This strange bird was seen more than once by the then parish clerk pecking from within at the grating, and furiously fluttering about within the enclosed vault. On another occasion it was seen by other people in the body of the church itself. The wife of the parish clerk and her daughter often saw it. The local bell-ringers, who all professed to deny its existence and appearance, one evening, however, came together to ring a peal, when they were told by a youth that the big raven was flying about inside the chancel. Coming together into the church with sticks and stones and a lantern, four men and two boys found it fluttering about amongst the rafters. They gave chase to it, flinging at it, shouting at and endeavouring to catch it. Driven hither and thither for some time, and twice or thrice beaten with a stick, so that one of its wings seemed to have been thus broken and made to droop, the bird fell down wounded with expanded wings, screaming and fluttering into the eastern part of the chancel, when two of the men on rushing towards it to secure it, and driving it into a corner, vaulted over the communion-rails, and violently proceeded to seize it. As the account stands, it at once sank wounded and exhausted on to the floor, and as they believed in their certain grasp, but all of a moment – vanished!

On 16 July 1883, the wife of Mr R.L. Burgh, who was sometime vicar of West Drayton, wrote to Revd Lee about the creature:

It was many years ago; and I had quite forgotten it until I got your note. I can remember feeling persuaded that a bird must have got into the family vault, and in going outside to look into it through the iron bars to try if anything could be seen there, the sounds were then always in the chancel in the same place.

Judging by other accounts, it seems that the legend of the spectral bird of West Drayton dated back further as there was mention of the winged wonder over fifty years prior to Revd Lee's account. It was believed by some of the local folk that the ghostly bird was in fact the soul of

A strange spectral bird haunted West Drayton church.

a local murderer who had taken his own life. In 1869 it was recorded that a lady and her sister, while visiting the church to lay flowers on the altar, had observed a huge black bird, which they believed must have escaped from the Zoological Gardens or some other private menagerie.

The Window-Tapping Magpie

Little is known about the ghostly magpie sighted at Great Russell Street, in London's West End. Vague records state that the phantom had been observed, usually between the hours of 2 and 3 a.m., tapping at windows with its beak and at one particular (unnamed) house. The bird also materialised in the bedroom, floating on a twig, before vanishing.

The Poultrygeist!

The story of Highgate's ghostly chicken is one of London's more quirky tales. It originates from 1626, when philosopher Sir Francis Bacon was travelling one wintry day with Dr Witherborne, friend and physician to James I. During their journey the gentlemen discussed Bacon's idea of preserving food by freezing, at which Witherborne scoffed. So, to prove a point, Bacon halted the carriage at Pond Square and ran to purchase a hen. Once prepared, he stuffed the chicken with snow, creating the world's first frozen chicken.

Unfortunately, Bacon died shortly afterwards of pneumonia, but it is not his spirit that haunts the area. Numerous reports have been made of a ghostly chicken wandering the square, its eerie shrieks heard on several occasions. The most documented case emerged during the Second World War when air-raid wardens often saw the phantom, with one man actually attempting to catch the ghost and eat it!

In 1943 a half-plucked chicken was seen on the road through Pond Square by a British airman and in the 1960s a motorist who had broken down was distracted by the bird, which

Pond Square – haunt
of the phantom
chicken!

vanished as he approached. But it seems that the last recorded sighting was in 1970 when a couple, cuddling in a doorway, observed the squawking apparition.

ETHEREAL BEARS

The Terror of the Tower

From the *Rochester Gazette & Weekly Advertiser*, Tuesday 15 November 1831 (No. 556, page 3):

> The king presented to the Zoological Society the entire contents of his menagerie, now deposited in the Tower [of London]. They amount to almost thirty in number and include four lions, three bears (the large bear is an extraordinary animal), one black wolf, three blood hounds, five leopards and three hyenas.

So, is it any surprise that one of the ghosts said to haunt Her Majesty's Royal Palace and Fortress is that of a bear? In 1815 a sentry on guard outside the Jewel Room was confronted by a monster of a bear, which came through the wall and headed straight for him. The guard reacted quickly and prodded his bayonet at the beast, only to see the blade glide through the apparition as if striking thin air. The phantom vanished, but the sentry was so traumatised by the experience that he was reported to have died shortly after the confrontation. Had the ghost simply been the spirit of a bear housed at the Tower menagerie, or was it a manifestation of many guises, for it was also recorded that a whitish, cylindrical vision appeared in the Jewel Room on one occasion, terrifying the Keeper of the Crown Jewels, a Mr Edmond Lenthal Swift, during the October of 1817. He was in the presence of his wife, their young son, and sister-in-law and eating a hearty meal in the sitting room of the Jewel House when Mrs Swift screamed, 'Good God, what is that?' and they all watched as a tubular phantom, the thickness of

The Tower of London, one of London's most haunted locations.

A phantom bear is said to haunt the Tower of London.

a man's arm, swirled around the table, until it approached Mrs Swift who screamed, 'Oh Christ! It has seized me!' Mr Swift attempted to strike the form, but his weapon hit the wall behind it as the spectre floated across the room and then vanished by the window.

The Chelsea Bears

The brown bear was wiped from the woods of Britain around the tenth century. However, the cruel sport of bear-baiting existed in England up until the nineteenth century. 'Bear-gardens' were constructed throughout the country from the sixteenth century and these pits would be circled by high seats so that spectators could observe the spectacle of a bear, usually chained to a post in the centre of the mini-arena, which would then have several, well-trained hunting dogs set upon it. Imagine the gory sight as these dogs were gradually killed, the bear also suffering appalling injuries before eventually being set free from its shackles in the ring to kill any other dogs that had been used to replace those killed.

The Paris Garden at Southwark was one of the most well-known bear-pits. It attracted around 1,000 people to each fight, even Queen Elizabeth I was in attendance on occasion. It is no wonder that the ghosts of bears have been seen not far from this location, at Cheyne Walk and Glebe Place, Chelsea. It seems that these local spectres appear in a variety of colours – black, brown and white – but, in general, spectral bears do not seem common across the United Kingdom, though reports do exist.

The Horror of Hackney Marshes

On 27 December 1981 four young boys were playing in the snow on Hackney Marshes when, they claimed, they were chased by a bear. Thirteen-year-old Tommy Murray said that, 'a giant, great growling hairy thing' had raised up on its hind legs and the boys had run away in terror. The witnesses were quick to tell their parents who in turn informed the local police, who, fifty in number and accompanied by dogs and a helicopter, scoured the marshes looking for the beast. Although they failed to flush out the creature, they did find a det of paw-prints in the snow; one set were spotted on an island which had a perimeter fence around it and a locked gate, and there were no human tracks nearby to suggest a hoax.

The Chief Inspector at the time commented, 'Although I didn't see the boys myself, I'm reliably informed that they were very frightened by what they saw. They were not hoaxers, although of course, they may have been hoaxed.'

An even more bizarre event occurred a year before at the River Lee (which runs from Luton in Bedfordshire to the River Thames), when two bear carcasses, both having been decapitated, were discovered. No one knew where the animals had come from.

The Wanstead Ewok

In the autumn of 2008, an eighteen-year-old fisherman named Michael Kent claimed to have encountered a bear-like beast while angling at Holiday Ponds, Wanstead.

Michael was heading off to a swim near where his brother was perched when a creature emerged from the shadows of the trees.

'I looked over and saw this strange, dark figure that resembled a bear. It was hunched over and I could see it had a really hairy back. I think it must have heard me and it scampered off ... It was too small to be a human, but not the right shape to be a deer, it didn't have long legs or anything like that,' said the witness.

Was the 'horror of Hackney Marshes' an escaped bear or a hoax?

Michael, despite the jokes from his brother and father, remained convinced he'd seen a bear, although park officials were quick to dismiss the report, stating matter-of-factly that only deer and foxes inhabited the area. However, Mr Kent responded, 'I've been fishing in the area since I was five years old, and I've seen deer, dogs and even a cow before, but never anything like this.'

Then, a few days later, pensioner Irene Daintly claimed to have seen a similar creature, commenting, 'It was about 4ft tall and with really big feet and looked straight at me with animal eyes. Then it leaped straight over the wall with no trouble at all and went off in the direction of the Three Jolly Wheelers pub.'

Bears rarely walk for long distances on two legs, and certainly don't leap over walls, but what had these two, seemingly reliable witnesses seen? The press at the time had a field-day, commenting that maybe something akin to Bigfoot was roaming the area!

HORSES FROM HELL

Throughout the UK, one of the most commonly sighted animal ghosts is that of the horse, especially when leading a spectral carriage.

On Bayswater Road, next to Hyde Park, a silent horse-bus is regularly sighted, while near Beddington, south London, the gallop of an invisible mare was often heard during the early 1930s. The phantom horse would apparently trot to the gates of Orchard House and then stop. The 'phantom coach of Enfield' is another example. This four-horse coach has been sighted since the eighteenth century, hovering slightly above the road on Bell Lane. Lord John Angerstein's coach has been sighted pulled by four headless horses in the vicinity of Trafalgar Road, travelling towards Vanbrugh Hill in south-east London. Why the horses are headless no one knows.

The huge gates of Black Horse Yard at Windsor are situated on the main Windsor to London road, which is flanked by houses built during the eighteenth century. It is here that an ominous apparition is said to appear before the death of a monarch. A ghostly coach pulled by two magnificent black horses rumbles from the shadows where an old inn once stood and travels towards Windsor Park. No one knows where the phantom goes for it fades into the gloom of the night before reaching its destination.

A spectral coach and horses. (Image created by Neil Arnold)

A phantom horseman. (Image created by Neil Arnold)

Rumour has it that the phantom carriage also harbours another ghost, that of the Royal Physician who was tending to King Charles II before his death. Sightings have yet to occur in modern times; legend states that the last time the spectre occurred Edward VII was gravely ill.

What is intriguing about spectral horses is how they often appear with spectral coaches, which suggests that somehow such inanimate objects have 'souls' too, for we rarely hear reports of a coachman gliding in mid-air.

Other common horse-related spectres include a horse ridden by a knight, seen at East Barnet. Meanwhile, a highwayman on horseback has been seen at Hampstead. Sightings of this phantom centre on Spaniards Inn, the famous pub associated with Dick Turpin, the notorious highwayman. Sources often cite Mrs Helen Steipel as an eyewitness to this spectre. She reported a ghostly highwayman charging at her from a thicket. After bracing for an impact that never came, she discovered that both rider and mount had vanished. Its hooves had made no sound.

Turpin's ghost moonlights at another location. The Rose and Crown, at Enfield, also claims the highwayman, who has been spotted riding past on a spectral Black Bess.

The ghost of a donkey is one of London's more unusual legends and its colourful, glowing form is said to appear at The Hyde, between Hendon and Kingsbury.

FIVE

A STRANGE LONDON SAFARI

The Spectral Ape of Hampstead

One of the most bizarre ghost stories from London is mentioned in ghost-hunter Elliot O'Donnell's 1954 book *Dangerous Ghosts*. The story revolves around a Mr Ward, a Hampstead man who, during the early 1900s, went to Sumatra on an expedition through the sweaty jungles. While there, he shot a pig-tailed macaque and was cursed by the woman who owned it. Local rumour was rife that the woman was a sorceress. Shortly after, Mr Ward was attacked and mauled by a tiger and was then stung by an insect, causing him so much pain that he returned to his London home.

After a few days back in London Mr Ward began to be tormented by a sinister apparition, that of a ghostly primate, which prowled his bedroom and leered at him every night. Friends of Mr Ward suggested that he may have been suffering from a fever and hallucinating, but after several terrifying encounters with the spectral ape, a close friend and a priest stood guard. One occasion, at around 1 a.m., Mr Ward screamed in horror and was found unconscious in his room. The priest crossed himself, despite the friend not seeing a thing.

'You do believe me now don't you?' asked the shivering Mr Ward after coming round.

A Hampstead resident was visited by a spectral ape.

'Something very terrible was in the room,' the priest exclaimed. 'I saw it very distinctly. It was simian just like you described it, Mr Ward, and very diabolical. It vanished as soon as I prayed. It won't trouble you again.'

After the mystifying encounter Mr Ward recovered, and was never plagued again by the creature.

The Brentford Griffin

On a summer's day in 1984, Kevin Chippendale was strolling along Braemer Road, Brentford, when something suddenly caught his eye flying near to the Green Dragon apartment building. Was it a bird? Or a plane? No, it was a griffin!

You may scoff at such a sighting, but for a short while the soaring oddity, which became known as the Brentford Griffin, remained one of London's most bizarre mysteries. And the sightings continued – Mr Chippendale saw the beast again in February of the following year, describing the monster as looking like a dog but with wings and having a long muzzle. Could it have been just a weird coincidence that his sighting had taken place so near to the aptly named Green Dragon building?

It wasn't just Kevin who spotted this creature. Angela Keyhoe (who knew Kevin) subsequently observed a large, black bird-like form perched on the gasometer next to the Waterman's Art Centre, and, to add credibility to the legend, a psychologist named John Olssen also saw the beaked creature while jogging alongside the Thames.

The eerie phantom was soon attracting media attention, with *The Six O'Clock Show* covering the sightings. However, the whole mystery was considered by many to be a hoax, especially after novelist Robert Rankin detailed the sightings and author Andrew Collins published a pamphlet on the enigma, *The Brentford Griffin: The Truth Behind The Tales*. Much of what was

The griffin – a mythological beast.

A griffin-like guardian perched on the Natural History Museum.

written, including eyewitness accounts, appears to have been fictional, but it seemed that the coverage of the beast had stirred too many imaginations. In other words, if you believe in something enough, it may actually start to happen. As Rankin admitted, 'We set up a griffin hotline, and people started ringing in. I thought, "Hang on a minute, even if this thing had no reality at first, it has now!"'

When we consider that Brentford's coat of arms features a Griffin, the local football team play at Griffin Park, and there is a pub called The Griffin in the town, should we consider the local monster as real or an imaginary creature moulded by local society who for decades had a winged wonder buried deep within its consciousness?

Now, while such a creature may well have been nothing more than fanciful rumour, it's worth noting a letter, submitted to *Fortean Times* magazine during May 1998, from Mr Martin Collins, who believed that such a monster may well have been more than local folklore. He wrote:

I first encountered the story of the Brentford Griffins while I was at St John's School in the 1950s. St John's in those days sat in the shadow of Brentford's football ground, Griffin Park. Inquiring why there were so many griffin references in Brentford, I was told that it was due to the family of griffins that lived on Brentford Eyot, an island in the Thames.

The story of how they got there was that the first griffin was brought to Brentford by King Charles II as a gift for his mistress, Nell Gwynn, who had a house in the Butts at Brentford. One day the griffin was playing on the banks of the River Brent, which flows past the Butts, and fell in. The hapless creature was washed down the Brent into the Thames, finally being washed up on Brentford Eyot. As it was assumed to have been killed, it was left alone and was able to live on the Eyot for many years – griffins having a lifespan of centuries.

Then Sir Joseph Banks brought back a griffin from a Pacific island where he had been with Captain Cook. This griffin was originally housed in the Pagoda in Kew Gardens, which is on the opposite bank of the Thames from Brentford Eyot where it found a mate awaiting it.

There was soon a whole colony of griffins and they spread out from the Eyot all over the town of Brentford, where they can still be seen to this day, if you look closely enough.

This story has stayed with me … it is a nice bit of Brentford mythology.

While intriguing and seemingly in support of the legend, these details simply prove how the creature had become symbolic within a community, just as dragons, satyrs, centaurs and other mythological beasts have the world over.

However, sightings of such winged monsters do still persist throughout the world and, while many of these reports describe griffin-like beasts, it seems that they could all be replicas of the more universal gargoyle figure seen perched above many a town throughout the world. This begs the question, are they merely stone guardians or echoes of what really lurks in the skies?

Zoologist Karl Shuker, when commenting on evidence of griffins in his book *From Flying Toads to Snakes with Wings*, said:

Relics purportedly from griffins – those fabulous monsters with the body of a lion but the head, wings and forequarters of an eagle – have also been documented. Their long talons were once highly prized, because they were reputedly able to detect poison and many were brought back to Western Europe by crusaders during the Middle Ages. Sadly, however, they invariably proved to be antelope horns, sold to the gullible fighters by African entrepreneurs. As noted by Edward Peacock (*The Antiquary*, September 1884), a griffin claw preserved in the British Museum is believed to be one of two contained in 1383 within the shrine of Saint Cuthbert, at Durham Cathedral. It resembles the horn of an ibex (a wild mountain goat).

Dragons over London?

Dragons are probably the most celebrated yet misunderstood of mythical creatures. Several sightings have been recorded and the monsters feature heavily in the lore of the British countryside (remember St George?) with tales of such frightful beasts appearing in the folklore of Sussex and Wales and across the world in Asia and Africa. During modern times such leviathans have been relegated to the league of fantasy, where they only exist alongside unicorns and fairies.

However, dragon-like 'sky serpents' have occasionally been seen over the capital and were first recorded in 1222. The Brentford Griffin, if genuine, was the last of the 'dragon' sightings. A similar yet smaller beast was spotted during the 1700s and mentioned in *The Gentleman's Magazine*:

In the beginning of the month of August, 1776, a phenomenon was seen in a parish a few miles west of London, which much excited the curiosity of the few persons that were so fortunate to behold it. The strange object was of the serpent kind; its size that of the largest common snake and as well as could be discovered from so transient a view of it, resembled by its grey, mottled skin. The head of this extraordinary animal appeared about the same size as a small woman's hand. It had a pair of short wings very forward on the body, near its head; and the length of the whole body was about 2ft. Its flight was very gentle; it seemed too heavy to fly either fast or high, and its manner of flying was not in a horizontal attitude, but with its head considerably higher than the tail, so that it seemed continually labouring to ascend without ever being able to raise itself much higher than 7 or 8ft from the ground.

Even more amazing was the fact that the magazine recorded, in 1797, another flying serpent account, this time between Hyde Park Corner and Hammersmith, on 15 June. The witness, merely known as 'J.R.', wrote a letter describing the weird encounter, stating:

The dragon – one of the most popular mythical monsters.

During the late 1700s flying serpents were seen between Hammersmith and Hyde Park.

... the body was of a dark colour, and about the thickness of the lower part of a man's arm, about 2ft long ... the wings were very short and placed near the head. The head was raised above the body. It was not 7 or 8ft above the ground.

While the creature seemed life-like, and indeed almost like a flying snake, the letter ended in morose fashion, concluding, '... being an animal of such uncommon description, I was particular in noticing the day of the month, and likewise being the day preceding a most dreadful storm of thunder and lightning.'

Mr Davy's Monster

It was a sunny day in October, the year 1878, when naturalist and London Aquarium employee Mr Davy exhibited his unusual beast, by taking it on an afternoon stroll.

Many onlookers gasped at the bizarre creature, which was most certainly unknown to science at the time and was described as 'a living cube'. It was 2ft in height and 2ft in length and bereft of abdomen and its rear two legs were situated almost directly behind its fore limbs. Its head was like that of a boar, as was the tail, and the body was covered in coarse hair. In *Land & Water* magazine the editor, Mr Buckland, who'd seen the traffic held up by the abomination, described the creature as a 'demon', although naturalist Thomas Worthington believed that such a beast might well have been a most unusual hyena.

Whatever the 'animal' was, it immediately caused outrage and hysteria. On one occasion, Mr Davy was so hounded and harassed that he fled into the bowels of an Underground railway station to escape his pursuers. Mr Davy then boarded an underground train, striking fear into the hearts of the passengers. Mr Davy also terrified his own landlord with his new pet; the man was sent fleeing in horror from his home.

While the beast never caused any harm, rumour had it that Mr Davy purchased the 'exotic' from some peasants while in southern France. Mr Davy told his friend, Mr Leman, that he knew nothing of the language and so was unable to find out where the beast had come from or what exactly it was.

The London Mermaid

The mermaid has long been confined to the menagerie of phantasmagoria. These 'mythological' creatures who inhabited old tales from sea travellers have stood the test of time, though are now portrayed as fantastic but fictional beings. But is there some truth behind the tales?

In 1822 American sea captain Samuel Barrett Eades took to London a fine specimen of a dried mermaid, which was exhibited (to much fuss) at the Turf coffeehouse at St James Street.

The creature had been bought by Eades from some Dutch fishermen who had received the bizarre form from Japanese fishermen, who had clearly not realised what kind of zoological wonder had sat before them. Eades had scraped together the money for his purchase by selling a ship named the *Pickering*, of which he owned one eighth, for $6,000 (although he failed to tell Mr Ellery, who owned the rest of the ship!).

Eades had then climbed aboard a vessel bound for London from Boston. When the boat temporarily anchored at Cape Town, Eades was quick to exhibit his specimen to enhance his

Mermaids feature heavily in folklore. But are they real?

funds. Many people gathered around the peculiar sight, with some claiming that they'd never seen such a wonder.

Dr Philip, representative of the London Missionary Society of Cape Town, wrote of the exhibit in a letter to the *London Philanthropic Gazette*, describing the beast, mentioning its baboon-like head with thin, black strands of hair. The chin, breasts, nose, fingers, eyes and nails resembled those of a human being and the body measured some 3ft in length. Belief was strong in its authenticity and when Eades arrived in London in 1822 he thought the world would be his oyster.

However, the creature was immediately confiscated from the captain – customs officers at the time were reluctant to release such a form, but after a short hiatus, Eades was on the road, looking for a theatre to display the mermaid and eventually rented a room at the Turf coffeehouse owned by a Mr Watson. An advertisement was drawn up for the exhibition, which read:

A MERMAID!!! – The wonder of the world, the admiration of all ages, the theme of the Philosopher, the Historian, the Poet … may be seen at number 59 St James Street every day, Sundays excepted, from ten in the morning until five in the afternoon. Admittance one shilling.

The public who flocked to see the sensation were not allowed to touch it, and it was protected by way of a glass dome. The *Mirror* at the time reported that some 400 people would visit the exhibit daily! Soon afterwards, the Eades mermaid was accepted as a novel species, and it was examined by a Dr Price, who exclaimed that the scholars of the sixteenth and seventeenth century had been correct in stating that mermaids did indeed exist.

However, Eades' bubble burst when Mr Ellery, owner of the *Pickering* ship, came to London, took Eades to court and proved that the mermaid was a fake. William Clift, an expert anatomist, after analyzing the mermaid, told the court how it had been manufactured. The cranium, hair and torso belonged to an orang-utan, the jaws and teeth were from a baboon, eyes and parts of skin were artificial, sawn human bones made up the limbs, the nails were constructed from horn and the main fish section of the creature had indeed come from a large fish. So, the specimen was a hoax.

The December issue of *The Gentleman's Magazine* revealed the truth: London's public had been conned. Eades, after spending so much money on it, was reluctant to give in and continued to display the specimen for want of small profit, but over time the audience and the interest shrivelled, just like the cleverly constructed skin of the mermaid. On 9 January 1823, the coffeehouse closed down.

The Markham Square Monster

At some time in the 1940s a gentleman was staying at Markham Square, Chelsea in order to visit his two sons. On the first night of his stay in a dingy room the man awoke with a sudden nightmarish jerk, and found himself face-to-face with a ghastly creature.

He later stated that:

> It was a dwarfed, tubby figure, with a face like a pig, perfectly naked, in a strong light. The whole figure resembled in appearance the scalded body of a pig, but the legs and arms were those of a human being brutalized; male or female, I could not say.

Within fifteen seconds the awful vision vanished, leaving the witness huddled and shaking under his sheets, sweat dripping profusely from his brow. The occasional bout of slumber provided no respite from the memory of the presence, and only the morning light erased what the witness believed was no nightmare.

The man discovered that a picture had fallen from a connecting door during the night, the noise of which may have been the reason for his awaking suddenly. However, no explanation was forthcoming on the pig-faced humanoid. No other such haunting was ever reported from the area, and the tale of the spectre was long forgotten … until now.

Such a hideous form may well have had its origins in the case of the Pig-Faced Lady, a deeply unfortunate woman who had a whole pamphlet dedicated to her in 1641, entitled *A Certain Relation of the Hog-faced Gentlewoman*. It read:

> The pig-faced lady, whose name is Tamakin Skinker, was born at Wirkham on the Rhine, in 1618. Some people assume she is English-born, being a native of Windsor-on-Thames. All the limbs and lineaments of her body is well featured and proportioned, only her face, which is the ornament and beauty of all the rest, has the nose of a hog or swine; which is not only a stain and blemish, but a deformed ugliness making all the rest loathsome, contemptible, and odious to all that look upon her. Her language is only the hoggish Dutch 'ough, ough', or the French

'owee, owee'. Forty thousand pounds is the sum offered to the man who will consent to marry her … She is now in London looking for a husband. She lives in Blackfriars or Covent Garden.

It is said that when she died, the tragic lady returned to haunt the area and was seen many years later by a man and his wife, who originally thought that they had burglars, until they encountered the apparition:

The footsteps became clearer, and there appeared before our eyes, at the top of the stairs, a lady in an old-fashioned dress – I should say probably early seventeenth century. Then she began to descend the stairs. Strange to say, she had the head of a pig, an ugly, repulsive pig – small eyes and snout complete. Well, down this horrible creature came – moving towards us. My wife screamed and then fainted. I managed to catch her as she fell. Looking up, my wife still in my arms, I observed with great pleasure that the terrible thing had vanished.

The Wolf of Clapham Common

A strange event occured on 22 February 1961, many centuries after wolves were said to prowl the woods of Richmond and Epping. Locals had been whispering of an unusual beast, like a big dog, grey in colour, with pointed ears lurking on Clapham Common. The Common itself is 220 acres and is situated between Clapham, Battersea and Balham. But is it big enough to hide a wolf?

Excited children and curious adults gathered in an area near St Paul's churchyard, which had been closed off by the police. A policeman armed with a loop and wearing strong gloves was leaning into a crevice between the churchyard and the adjacent hostel. Inching ever nearer to the creature that no one else could see but only imagine, he slipped the noose over the beast. Tragically, the creature was far from being a fearsome, growling monster and was so traumatised by the event that its heart failed on the spot, and it died.

Indeed it had been a wolf, said to have escaped from confinement and one of a pair that had been kept by a local woman in an inadequately fenced closure. Despite the panic, many children cried for the wolf.

King Rat

It is said that in London you're never more than 5ft away from a rat at all times, a rather ghastly statistic if ever there was one. So consider the legend of the King Rat, a monstrous creature mentioned in Bob Rickard and John Michell's fascinating book *Living Wonders*:

Workers in London sewers tell of rare sightings of the King Rat, a huge creature, paler than the rest, attended by a bodyguard of other large rats. On his appearance the ordinary rats become silent and motionless.

A scary thought indeed that some monstrous rodent lurks beneath our city conducting armies of thousands of pesky vermin to take to our streets.

Do monster rats lurk in the
sewers of London?

Weirder than a Flying Womble!

To end this chapter, something even weirder from the phantom menagerie and located in the last place you'd expect high levels of strangeness – Wimbledon!

This is the peculiar case of the flying squirrel of Wimbledon Common, a tale which featured in the 3 October 2008 edition of the *Wimbledon Guardian*:

Walkers on Wimbledon Common could be forgiven for thinking they are nuts following reports of a mystery mammal. According to eyewitnesses a strange animal similar to a squirrel is hiding out on the common, leaving people wondering what kind of beast it could be. So far educated guesses on website Wild About Britain have included the Australian sugar glider, the North American flying squirrel or another species of possum. Rather more tongue in cheek suggestions have included a flying womble – on account of the common being home to the fictional television characters.

Wandsworth's Kolin Barnz, who spotted the beast while on the commons, said, 'It was squirrel-like but its face looked more mouse-like, with long whiskers, black eyes and small ears. As it jumped between trees, flaps of skin stretched between its front and back legs and it glided to the next tree. I couldn't believe my eyes. How the animal got to its new home is anyone's guess, but it is possible it could be someone's escaped pet.

And finally, we've even covered yarns pertaining to flying serpents over the capital. But pink jellyfish? The *Wimbledon Guardian* covered the weird story on 9 January 2009, when a visitor to the newspaper office stated quite categorically that he'd seen an object over Merton.

'I looked out of my flat window this morning, and to my surprise noticed a large bright pink jellyfish-looking object surrounded by a pink haze. It appeared to be hovering over or above the pylons in the distance.'

Wimbledon – home of the wombles and unidentified flying objects!

The witness and the paper attempted to make some kind of connection between the object and the Merton Abbey turbine, at the shopping centre, especially when five days previously it was alleged that a 'UFO' had hit a turbine in Lincolnshire.

A spokesman for the shopping centre, however, commented that no aliens or unusual flying creatures had been seen in the area, despite the fact that strange objects had indeed been seen over Wimbledon the previous year. Now, UFOs are one thing, but a pink jellyfish really takes the biscuit, doesn't it?

SIX

CLOSE ENCOUNTERS OF THE LONDON KIND

Early Invaders

Whether driven by martians or related to the human psyche we'll never know, but unidentified flying objects are very much part of our sub-culture and claims about UFO sightings have been with us a lot longer than we realise. Anecdotal evidence from the year 664 suggests a weird green light was observed by some nuns, which appeared at Barking and headed over London. In 764 many 'dragons' were seen over the UK, including London, and in 1593 there is brief record of a 'flying dragon surrounded by flame' over the city. Meanwhile, in 1741, a 'fireball' was observed over Kensington by Lord Beauchamp, but it measured only eight inches in diameter. One year later at St James Park, a rocket-like ship was observed for many minutes by a Fellow of the Royal Society.

In 1882 astronomer Walter Maunder observed what could well have been one of the most impressive UFO incidents related to the capital. While peering into the vast abyss of space from Greenwich Observatory, Walter was startled to see a disc-like object, greenish in colour, moving at phenomenal speed across the sky, heading in a north-easterly direction. Shortly afterwards in *The Observatory* magazine, the Royal Astronomical Society asked researchers to write down

A visitor from outer space. (Courtesy of Alan Friswell)

the most amazing things they'd seen through telescope, to which Maunder responded with an article on the bizarre flying object.

Scareships

Long before the First World War, Germany manufactured a number of Zeppelin airships, but several failed test flights meant that it wasn't until 1908 that the invention took off. However, a spate of phantom airship sightings around the same time suggested a fleet of ships of unknown origin were buzzing the skies. As only twenty-one airships were manufactured prior to the First World War, could some of these ships actually have been UFOs? Some crafts seemed to vanish into thin air or mysteriously escape from pursuits. Here is a chronicle pertaining to the capital:

9 May 1909 – 11 p.m.: A mystery object with flashing lights was seen over London. The craft had two searching spotlights and was estimated as travelling at 210mph!

13 May 1909 – 11.10 p.m.: A Mr Graham and a Mr Bond were returning from Teddington to Richmond, south-west London when they heard a buzzing noise. They observed a 250ft-long ship creeping along the surface of the grass of Ham Common and liaised with two strange-looking pilots who gave them a pipe!

14 May 1909 – 3.30 a.m.: Two railway shunters working in Tottenham saw a craft shaped like a policeman's truncheon that headed towards Downhill Park. The object was unlit and moved without sound.

25 February 1913: Prime Minister Mr Asquith met aviator Claude Graeme-White to discuss the air-scare.

24 August 1914 – 7.30 p.m.: An object resembling an enemy airship was seen by observers at Hendon Aerodrome. At 8.45 p.m., possibly the same or a very similar ship was seen over the mouth of the Thames.

28 August 1914 – 1.15 a.m.: A surgical radiographer from Brixton heard the whirring noise of propellers and saw two strong beams of light search in the background.

5 September 1914 – 9.05 p.m.: Police patrolling the River Thames by boat close to Woolwich Arsenal saw a huge egg-shaped object pass over their boats.

8 September 1914 – 7.15 p.m.: Two peculiar and very large phantom airships were seen over Brixton. An aircraft was sent out to investigate the sighting but found no sign of the craft.

27 September 1914 – 2 a.m.: An airship was seen over Bromley.

7 November 1914 – 7 p.m.: Police officers watched a huge airship over London.

Phantom airships and UFOs have been seen over Bromley.

1 February 1915: Five Zeppelin ships headed over London and then seemed to vanish. Other ships were also reported in winds so strong that such ships should have found it impossible to take to the air. In the previous year there had been over 500 reports of phantom airships in the UK.

September 1915: Rumours circulated that an airship had crashed on Hampstead Heath, with one witness bringing horses to carry away the wreckage. Amidst sinister rumours and paranoia, two more airships were sighted over London in this month, both disappearing before the eyes of pilots.

The Early Twentieth Century

During February 1934 at Dollis Hill, north-west London, a married couple watched in amazement as two men wearing caps appeared to tend to a cylindrical craft situated on the ground near their home. The brave couple decided to approach, but suddenly the craft moved away and there was no sign of the men.

In 1937 at an unnamed location in the capital, but during broad daylight, an eight-year-old girl strolling through a meadow encountered a bizarre flying object that hovered above her. Suddenly, a platform descended from the craft and men, dressed in red, emerged and took her on board the ship. The girl noted that the inside of the craft was extremely large which didn't seem apparent from the outside and that once she was seated in a chair she was faced by a bright light, which in turn enabled her to experience strange visions. After this she was taken in the craft to a large pyramid in an unknown place, and after walking through a dark corridor she emerged back into the meadow where she was picked up!

This case hints at the 'alien abduction' phenomenon which would later pepper the lore of Ufology, but it would be another decade before the 'UFO age' took over, culminating in thousands of worldwide sightings, hysteria, news coverage and government interest.

The Coming of the Saucers

The UFO craze hit the headlines from the 1940s onwards. For London, it was 22 November 1947 when a female witness, while under hypnosis, spoke of being abducted by two silver-suited females and put before a man who burned the figures 'H6AQ' onto her leg, which were still visible when she awoke from her trance.

On 5 February 1948 another UFO witness under hypnosis recalled being drawn towards a conical-shaped craft, where she encountered a tall man and small, egg-headed beings. In July 1953, at an unnamed London location, a twelve-year-old boy blacked out on a school trip. Under hypnosis he revealed that he'd seen a light in the sky, was unable to move and then was approached by two figures that were small, greyish in colour, and had large eyes. The boy received telepathic messages from the humanoids and was floated into a craft, where he met a figure adorned in red who claimed to be the boy's father. The boy was then shown a screen depicting the Earth and then led to a room full of children, and a woman, who took his silver crucifix, told him, '… it's not right to worship'. The boy soon passed out and was awoken by his teacher.

In 1954 at Chelsea, Air Marshal Peter Horsley claimed that he'd been invited by a General Martin to the home of a Mrs Markham. However, upon arrival, he was greeted by an extraterrestrial being named Mr Janus who spoke of space travel. When Horsley returned to the apartment, it was empty!

With regards to their importance and impact, the *London Sunday Dispatch* described UFOs as '… bigger than the Atom Bomb wars'.

The Cosmic Sixties

Newspapers across the world were being bombarded by UFO reports by the time the 1950s came to an end. The more spiritual '60s were no exception. On 15 July 1963 a farmer from Charlton found a crater measuring 2½m wide and the same deep on his land. Around the hole were four impressions, as if something had stood or landed there and the soil and foliage surrounding the hole were scorched.

Weird lights were seen over the capital, heading for Epping and on 27 December 1963, an odd, white craft was seen in fields at Epping.

On 15 August 1967, at 2.10 a.m., a male witness in North London visiting the bathroom glanced out of the window and noticed a dazzling, stationary object, at eye-level, just 500 yards away. Two smaller lights suddenly shot out from the bright object, and then the larger light began to wobble and rise. The object moved towards the man, losing its dazzle and appearing as pear-shaped. The craft went over the house and the man was able to see that its underside was constructed of thousands of tiny lights – yet despite its sheer size there was no sound.

After the initial shock and excitement, the witness called the police, who logged the call. Later the man noticed that the right side of his face, his hands and right arm had browned and become flaky.

According to the witness, others had seen the craft, and all, including him, were taken by private vehicles to the Ministry of Defence in London to discuss and sketch what they'd seen.

Although the unnamed location of the sighting was sectioned off for a while due to the discovery of unusual impressions in the soil, nothing more was heard about the incident and the witness made a recovery from wounds said to have been caused by ultra-violet radiation.

Did a UFO leave a strange impression in Charlton in 1963?

In the summer of 1967 in South London, three witnesses described encountering a black craft with a luminous yellow glow hovering around 5ft from the ground. The object suddenly descended, beaming an orange light to the soil, and out of the craft there appeared a hairless humanoid with webbed hands. It soon re-entered the object, which then took off.

At around the same time one of London's most impressive UFO sightings took place and was witnessed by thousands across the south-east. It was 7 p.m. on a clear night when a man spotted the oval-shaped object. It was travelling low, at around 4,000ft, and straight, but not at great speed, and it had a multi-colouration as it throbbed. Others watched the object as it went over a cloud, giving off an amazing electric lightshow. Witnesses believed that the craft would have been picked up on radar at Heathrow.

After the sighting, television, radio and newspaper channels were bombarded with calls as the craft moved south, and the story made the front page of the *Mirror*.

A group of teenagers formed the Enfield UFO Investigation Society after a spate of sightings in the mid-1960s.

One year later, at Stratford, a witness had just finished supper when she looked outside and noticed a figure of around 5ft in height in her yard. The humanoid had goat legs, was covered in dark fur and had green eyes and a long muzzle. Although it appeared malevolent, the witness, for some time after the incident, felt enlightened, as though she'd gained more wisdom telepathically from the creature. Nothing more was heard from the satyr-like manifestation.

Strangeness in the Seventies

The 1970s began slowly for UFO reports over the capital, but then things got very weird! Firstly a witness at Acton reported a UFO sighting to Hounslow police station. Then, two police officers in the same building spotted what was presumably the same craft and watched it with binoculars. The craft was circular and bright but showing black spots. A Scotland Yard spokesperson confirmed the sightings.

Then, in 1975 near Erith, a male witness saw an object shaped liked an airship that drifted over south-east London. It was a brightly lit, orange craft, which the witness observed for more than five minutes.

The year 1977 started oddly. During January a man in an unnamed location of London saw a crackling orb in the sky and then caught a fleeting glimpse of a 3ft tall, yellow humanoid which glided over the ground.

The 1977 Hainault Forest incident is one of the most bizarre UFO cases, but surprisingly it has been pretty much overlooked by many investigators over the years. On 5 May in this London Borough, two police officers saw a huge red light moving near the woodland lake. The object was only 300 yards away when it completely vanished. The officers bravely approached the spot where it had disappeared and one of them spotted a strange white craft, which also suddenly vanished. The only trace left of the objects was a strong burning smell.

On 8 May at 7 p.m., two men parked up in a marshy, heavily wooded area known as Cabin Hill, in the forest. They took a stroll with their dogs but were alerted to a rustling noise in the bushes. To their horror, they were approached by an 8ft tall, 4ft wide blue figure that suddenly vanished into the woods.

E.T. & the Eighties

During the mid to late 1980s reports of alien abductions were spreading like wildfire across the world, and it appeared as though the abductors had taken on their latest, slim-line form – being large-headed, bug-eyed and slender extraterrestrials (known as 'greys' or 'grays') keen on paralysing witnesses and performing various surgical procedures on them, from impregnation to the insertion of strange microchips. However, some encounters also involved other entities that harked back to the 1950s when B-movie type spectres were roaming our bedrooms.

In 1986 in London one October night, a man was awoken by small beings that were blue in colour and had the ability to flit through walls. The humanoids wore gowns like that of a surgeon and performed several sinister operations on the victim by way of extracting blood from his index finger and also touching him with a rod that had a glass ball at the end, which caused him so much pain that he passed out. When he awoke there was no sign of the intruders.

On 6 October 1986, also in the capital, a woman dying of cancer was visited by short, grey humanoids wearing strange helmets who lifted her up onto the ceiling. Four years previously, in Wembley, Lorraine Parry was walking through the neighbourhood one evening when, suddenly, she entered some surreal time slip and her surroundings altered dramatically into a desert-like terrain. Then, around her appeared a lake and a craft whizzed through the sky, its metallic surface glinting. Peculiar figures from inside the craft were gazing out from the windows and pointing at her excitedly.

On 31 March 1989 a strange craft landed in a field next to a busy road in the capital. A police officer was called to the scene and approached the object hesitantly, when suddenly a silver-suited humanoid appeared. The policeman didn't initially realise it but he'd been the victim of a hoax perpetrated by businessman Richard Branson, who'd intended to fly the disguised hot-air balloon to Hyde Park on 1 April but had been blown off course.

The Nineties and Beyond

In July 1991 a Boeing 737 waiting to land at Gatwick Airport had a strange encounter with an unidentified craft. The object was captured on radar. This incident echoed that of a Concorde, which, in 1979, had a close call with a reddish object which appeared to buzz over the plane at Heathrow and was observed by witness Mrs Godden, who stated that the craft seemed to be heading straight for the plane but seemed to travel straight through it.

A male witness at an unnamed location in London claimed he was awoken one night by a strange shaft of light which appeared in his room. Then, two mysterious beings, grey in colour, beckoned him as they waved a peculiar blue light at him.

At Hayes in 1995 a woman and her son watched a huge, black, triangular craft which appeared in the sky above their house. The following year, on 18 October at Walthamstow, two young children were alerted to an object in the sky after hearing a 'tish-tish' sound. The object they saw was orange in colour and hovered over their bedroom. Two years later, also at Walthamstow, a huge, boomerang-shaped craft was observed through binoculars by a local witness.

Fast forward to 2004 and there was a bizarre encounter involving a man only known as 'Jim', who stated that he was awoken on 16 January at his London home by a clicking noise. Suddenly, Jim was confronted by a freakish humanoid which stood around 5ft in height but had a head like a praying mantis. The creature seemed to have telepathic powers and sent Jim all manner of confusing messages which were distracted by bright lights. After a few minutes the being vanished, leaving a trail of purple vapour.

In the same year UFO investigator Nick Pope stated that Streatham and Lewisham were the hottest areas in London regarding UFO activity after a poll was conducted. The locations were tenth in the league of the UK's most likely places to see a UFO.

In 2006 many witnesses claimed to have seen a strange figure resembling an angel in the vicinity of the Thames. This wasn't the first sighting of the 'angel' either. An etching from 1865 shows a winged human floating over the river, and it was observed by many witnesses working at the Embankment at the time. In 1914 a photograph taken at Southwark docks, after the outbreak of the First World War, was said to show an angel. However, in reality the picture shows nothing more than a faint blur. The same could also be said for a photograph with a similar claim that was taken in August 1918 not far from the vicinity of Cleopatra's Needle.

UFOs over London. (Illustrated by Adam Smith)

The River Thames, where an angel has been seen.

Researchers who have devoted time to this phenomenon believe the first ever sighting of the 'angel', although based on unreliable accounts, originates from around 1667, a year after the Great Fire of London. Since then there have been over thirty sightings of this alleged figure, although some would argue that what is being seen is nothing more than a reflection of light or illusion.

During the sixth century it was recorded that several fishermen rowing beside the south bank of the Thames were approached by a hooded, monk-like figure who requested to be taken across the river. As the journey was completed it was said that the newly built church, dedicated to St Peter, became illuminated and the sky above filled with angels.

Many cases of weird lights in our skies or strange discs hovering in the zenith, can often be explained by natural phenomena, such as clouds, or terrestrial objects such as planes, Chinese lanterns, helicopters, and weather balloons. However, despite the scepticism, strange and often unexplainable objects are still reported each year over the capital.

SEVEN

A HANDFUL OF HAUNTINGS

London is one of the world's most haunted cities. Here are a few classic spine-chillers for the fireside, for no paranormal book should be without its ghosts.

The House at Berkeley Square

No. 50 Berkeley Square, W1, is arguably London's most famous haunted house. Some of the residents to have lived on the street include William Pitt, the Earl of Chatham (No. 6), Horace Walpole (No. 11) and Lord Clive (No. 45, which is where he committed suicide in 1774). The house has also been the address of the antiquarian booksellers, Maggs Brothers.

A certain Mr Myers occupied No. 50 for many years; he had bought the house and was due to move in with his fiancée when she changed her mind at the last minute and jilted him. Mr Myers was left to live in the house by himself. He lived in a small top room as a hermit and once in a while his shadow could be seen through the curtains as he moved around his room during the late hours. The only company he ever had was his manservant, and he never allowed a woman to enter his house.

After Mr Myers's death, the house often stood quite empty. During the late 1870s the house became notorious for its ghost sightings, which were said to have taken place in the small top room.

Mayfair magazine of 1879 commented:

This is known as the haunted house in Berkeley Square. It appears that the house had an evil character for being badly haunted so long ago as when it was last lived in – that is to say, once upon a time. One day a maidservant, newly arrived, was put to sleep in one of the upper rooms. An hour or two after the household was at rest, it was awakened by fearful screams from the new servant's room, and she was found standing in the middle of the floor, rigid as a corpse, with hideously glaring eyes – she had suddenly become a hopeless and raving mad woman, who never found a lucid interval wherein to tell what had made her so.

Many scoffed at the legends, but there were a few souls who were too afraid of venturing into the house in case they should see something that would cause them to die of fright.

A Lord Lyttleton spent the night in this top room on one occasion, accompanied only by two shotguns. One of these was indeed fired at some kind of movement in the darkness, but what exactly this movement was was not discovered.

Number 50, Berkeley Square.

A Mr Bentley took lease of the house with his two daughters and immediately noted the strange, musty smell, which reminded him of the animal cages at the local zoo. The eldest of Mr Bentley's daughters was engaged to a Captain Kentfield, who took a short stay at the house. The night before his arrival, the maid busied herself preparing a room for him when suddenly she screamed, 'Don't let it touch me!' The family rushed to her aid and found her collapsed on the floor. She died the next morning in hospital.

Captain Kentfield duly arrived the next day, unperturbed by the unfortunate event of the previous night. After settling down for a mere thirty minutes, his pistol shots and screams rang clear through the house. Kentfield was found dead, his face frozen in a look of utmost horror.

However, the most well-known and terrifying event concerned two sailors who, after a night out in the local pubs, decided to test the legend of the then derelict building by occupying a room at the top of the building. The sailors broke into the house, but after only being settled for a short time they were plagued by loud bangs and the patter of footsteps through the house. Suddenly, the steps reached the outside of the room they were occupying and the door flew open and there, before them, was a shapeless horror beyond imagination. One of the petrified sailors fled, rushing past the unfathomable terror and leaving his friend behind. The next day the sailor who'd fled, accompanied by a policeman, went back to the house, and there they found the body of the other sailor impaled on the railings below the window of the reputedly haunted room. It appeared that he'd leapt to his death in an attempt to escape whatever grotesque fiend had entered the room.

The Woman in Black

The Woman in Black stage show at the Fortune Theatre, on Russell Street in Covent Garden, is one of the most terrifying spectacles you are likely to witness. For those of you who are

The Fortune Theatre, Covent Garden.

The Woman in Black is a chilling stage play.

Several actors have seen a ghost in the theatre.

not familiar with this chilling ghost story, it is an adaptation of Susan Hill's book of the same name and has been running in the West End since 1989, and remains the longest running show second only to Agatha Christie's *The Mousetrap*.

Susan Hill's atmospheric book was made even more chilling in 1990 when it appeared on television as a Christmas Eve ghost tale and scared many who were not expecting such a sinister tale. The film, although slightly different from the book, which had strong echoes of some of the BBC's adaptations of M.R. James' classic spooky tales, remains one of the most unnerving supernatural programmes ever shown.

The Fortune Theatre itself is rumoured to be haunted in the truest sense by several apparitions. It seems that these few wandering spirits only reared their phantom heads after the play began its long-running stint. Previous members of the cast, including Sebastian Harcombe, experienced two strange episodes. The first was several years ago when the ghastly apparition of the story appeared during the first graveyard scene. Sebastian, looking towards the woman in black, saw two figures instead of one on the right of the stage. The actress at the time also mentioned that she'd been followed as she made her way to the stage. Sebastian also saw a grey figure, possibly a woman, lurking in one of the lower boxes of the theatre.

The Ghost Bus

That vehicles can appear as apparitions has long been confirmed by sightings across the capital of the already mentioned carriages pulled by spectral horses, and yet one modern-day mode of transport is said to haunt Cambridge Gardens, Notting Hill Gate in the west of London.

The most recent report of what has become known as the 'ghost bus' was recorded in 1990. The vehicle is said to be a number seven double-decker, which has been observed around 1.15 a.m. during the month of May each year. Most sightings of the ghost bus have involved other motorists who have had to swerve to avoid the approaching double-decker.

The first sighting on record was said to have taken place in 1934, when a man driving along Cambridge Gardens swerved to avoid the bus. His car crashed, killing him instantly. Some witnesses at the time of the accident reported that the victim had attempted to avoid a bus, while a handful of other observers claimed the man swerved for no reason, and saw no bus approaching.

Those who have had the terrifying experience of seeing the bus while driving, report that no driver is at the helm and in the early hours of the morning the bus never has its lights on. The vehicle races along the road, heading straight for oncoming motorists, who, once they've avoided the bus, turn around to look and are astonished when they see no bus rumbling further down the road.

Why such a vehicle haunts the area of Cambridge Gardens we will never know, but perhaps they exist to either cause accidents or to make motorists swerve to avoid them. It seems that the phantom bus never stops, but then again, who would want to step aboard this devilish double-decker?

A Happening at Brockley Road

In the borough of Lewisham sits Brockley Road, a location not exactly known for its unnerving apparitions. However, during the 1800s an article was posted to a magazine known as the *Review of Reviews* (which was edited by Mr W.T. Stead, who would unfortunately perish aboard the *Titanic* in 1912). The case concerned a seemingly haunted house. The usual strange things had taken place, such as footsteps in the night, shadowy figures, the opening of doors, and the feeling of being watched. However, the most unsettling incident to occur at the house involved a woman, who, during one summer evening was walking along a corridor looking for something when her attention was drawn to a strange glowing object in the darkest corner. The object seemed to be a small light but, as she approached, she was aware that the colouration was an intensifying yellowish-green. Suddenly, she could pick out a hideous face, with awful green, staring eyes that seemed to sparkle and a scrawny mass of matted hair. Although transfixed by the fiendish head, the woman muttered, 'In the name of Christ, be gone!' Thankfully, the terrifying wraith dissipated into the darkness.

In the same street there was much fuss made about another haunted residence, a home prowled by a tall, dark shade wearing a top-hat who often crouched in the doorway. The same house was also known for its ghoul that was often said to be able to open locked doors at night and torment those in slumber with its strange behaviour.

Rumours spread at the time that a murder had been committed at the house – a man killed by burglars. It is said that his spirit loiters forever more in this place.

Spirits of Sutton House

Sutton House at Hackney (built in 1535 and in the care of the National Trust) is most certainly a haunted building. In 1990 an architect staying at the premises encountered a ghostly blue lady while he was lying in bed. The figure hovered above him. This appears to be a rather aggressive spectre as it also apparently shook the bed of a house steward recently.

The ghost of a man in a top-hat haunts Brockley Road. (Illustration by Adam Smith)

A white phantom lady also haunts the place and is said to be the deceased wife of John Machell, who once owned the house. She died during childbirth in the house during the 1570s.

However, the eeriest spirits which the house harbours are spectral dogs. These also date back to the middle of the 1500s when Mr Machell, who was then a wealthy wool merchant, owned such animals. Their banshee-like wails are often said to reverberate around the rooms, especially at night.

Dogs are emblazoned on the family coat of arms, and anyone who visits the house with their own dogs are sure to be in for a surprise, for it is often noted how such animals act rather strangely as if in the presence of some unseen entity. The ghostly dogs are presumed to loiter at the top of the staircase for it is at the bottom of the stairs that visiting dogs sit and refuse to go any further, while staring wildly up the flight.

Ghosts of Baker Street

Baker Street, which lies in the Marylebone area of West London, is famous for its Sherlock Holmes connections – the great detective would no doubt have found the many hauntings of this famous street a fine mystery indeed. For Baker Street has long been considered the capital's most haunted street, harbouring a true gaggle of phantoms, spooks and spectres to chill the bones on a dark night.

The old Kenwood House Hotel has a variety of ghosts to speak of, the most unusual being a piece of furniture said to have drawers which open and shut of their own accord. Researchers have claimed in the past that the mirrored window of the fine piece is indeed possessed by a poltergeist of sorts. The hotel is also haunted by a gentleman who resembles a Cavalier.

A ghostly figure is said to loiter in The Volunteer public house. It is said to have connections to the Nevill family, who owned a house (which unfortunately burnt down in 1654) on the site the pub now occupies. Rupert Nevill is said to haunt the cellar.

Other ghosts of the street are fleeting, one being that of actress Sarah Siddons, who lurks in the electrical substation at 228 Baker Street, where her house once stood.

Why such spirits remain here has never been fully explained. Maybe some phantoms return here after death to continue an existence of sorts in a place they once loved. Or perhaps such ghosts are trapped in limbo, forever doomed to walk a void between the real and ethereal?

Haunting at Hampton Court

London's dark history is littered with tales of eerie mysteries, and not many places harbour such spectral presence as Hampton Court Palace, the most haunted royal residence in the capital. Located next to the River Thames to the south-west of London and stretching for over sixty acres, this beautiful estate has been shared with the public since 1838, and many of these visitors are aware of the spectres which reside within the vast hallways and beneath the beams.

Cardinal Thomas Wolsey built the palace in 1514, but in 1528 it was Henry VIII who took over the place and it was here that his second wife, Anne Boleyn, was accused of adultery and eventually beheaded in the Tower of London. Her ghost, adorned in a blue dress, is said to haunt both the Tower and the corridors of Hampton Court, and she remains one of London's most famous spooks.

In 1887 a three-year-old boy drowned in the small lake of the property and in 1927 a couple visiting the palace were horrified when their daughter, also aged three, ran into the lake and vanished beneath the depths. The same incident occurred in 1967 when a four-year-old boy ran into the water, but on this occasion he was saved. However, when asked why he'd chosen to run into the water, he replied, '... to play with the other children!'

Another young spirit also haunts the place, that of an eight-year-old page boy. The ghosts of the place are numerous. Some of the more often mentioned specres include the group of two men and seven women who vanished in front of a policeman in 1917 as he opened the front gate for them, a grey lady, and also the apparitions of two Cavaliers said to have haunted an area close to the Fountain Court. Their presence was a mystery until a sewage worker found their remains beneath a pathway.

Exhibit 22542

When ancient tombs were disturbed in Egypt, legends of fatal curses spread like wildfire. Whether such whispers were true or whether any tragedies surrounding such excavations were mere coincidence, the case of Exhibit 22542 at the British Museum may warn us not to take such sinister rumours lightly.

The item in question is a mummy discovered in the latter part of the 1800s which, over time, harboured such an awful reputation that it was even blamed for the start of the First World War! The Egyptian mummy-case of a singer to the priesthood of Amen-Ra has allegedly caused thirteen deaths, although hardened sceptics would argue otherwise.

The worst tragedy occurred when the mummified body was shipped to America in the early 1900s and the boat, the *Empress of Ireland*, sank at St Lawrence. Then, in 1921, two psychics attempted to exorcise the alleged curse which was bestow upon whoever should move or even

The British Museum.

Exhibit 22542 – the cursed mummy-case.

touch it. Legend has it that the two psychics were able to contact the familiar spirit which was said to act as a guardian to the mummy, and were appalled by its appearance, which resembled a floating jellyfish.

Such is the fear instilled by the case and its occupier, that many have claimed simply touching or photographing the mummy will cause misfortune, death or profuse bleeding from unseen wounds while in its vicinity.

Strange Feelings at Ealing

A photographer, keen to set up his own studio, moved into a half-derelict house, bringing with him his staff, who, although slightly unnerved by the setting, settled in comfortably. That is until the noises started.

The peculiar noises came from unoccupied rooms, sounds of the shifting of furniture when no one was around. Members of staff also began to sense a presence, an unseen hand which tapped them on the shoulder or tugged at their garments, and spectral voices from within the walls soon made this an awkward place to reside.

The photographer had a strong interest in the paranormal, as had many of his staff, and so, one evening as darkness drew in, they decided to hold a séance in the hope of communicating with the dead. To their delight, they did indeed contact a spirit, but the eerie presence spoke of unrest in the neighbouring building, a place that had seen much evil within its walls. A lady and her very young child had been butchered in the property, and a man, belonging to one of the forces, was accused, found guilty and hanged for his crime. It was during this detail that the photographer began to feel sore around his neck, and felt that the spirit in contact with them was in fact the alleged murderer, and this was confirmed when the spectre pleaded its innocence.

Whether such an apparition was cast from the property we'll never know,;only further experiences can shed some light on as to whether the property is still haunted.

The Enfield Poltergeist

Throughout London's history and ghost lore, the case of the Enfield Poltergeist remains one of the most bizarre. Between 1977 and 1979 this haunting was investigated by one Maurice Grosse who, two years previously, had lost his daughter in a crash. He felt that the Enfield mystery was meant for him, but little did he realise just how potent and everlasting the story would remain.

The three-bedroom semi-detached house was owned by single parent Peggy Hodgson, who lived there with her four children. Eleven-year-old Janet was the first to notice odd knocking noises, but such disturbances were considerably minor in comparison to what was about to occur. Larger objects in the house began to be pushed around, doors slammed, windows opened and loud banging noises reverberated around the home, alarming the children more and more as they intensified. Then, the unknown shifter of objects dealt a violent blow to one of the young children, a small boy. When WPC Caroline Heaps visited the house, she was shocked to see a chair floating in the middle of a room. Then, things got worse as the children, particularly young Janet, were attacked in their beds, strangulation was attempted, bed sheets were strewn and Peggy's nine-year-old son Billy had a lucky escape when an iron grate crashed onto his bed as he slept, thrown by an invisible assailant.

Despite the serious nature of the incidents, many locals believed the 'ghost' to be nothing more than a hoax perpetrated by the family, but the Society of Psychical Research suggested something unknown was to blame. When Janet and her sister Margaret began speaking in demonic tongue, the case took a disturbing turn. Pools of water began appearing throughout the house, and in the end more than fifteen separate cases were witnessed by many people.

Why Janet was singled out we'll never know, but investigators believed that it was the spirit of an old man who had died in the house which may have caused the torment. His name was Bill Hobbs and he is buried in Durant's Park graveyard. Unfortunately for Peggy Hodgson, she had to put up with the awful phenomenon until one day it suddenly ceased, never to return.

Curse of the Nurse

One night in 1943, the air raids had been particularly severe over London, and so the following day it wasn't unusual for workman Charles Bide to be sent off to various crumbling and damaged abodes to retrieve furniture that had survived the Blitz. On this occasion his boss sent him to St Thomas's Hospital.

Upon arrival he noticed that inside the building there seemed to be an unnatural coldness, although he thought nothing more of it and made his way through the rooms in search of furniture to secure. Only the sound of his own footsteps echoed through the building and when he reached the top floor freezing spots seemed to appear. It was then that he glimpsed the mirror …

It had been undamaged by the raids and, as he approached, he was terrified to see that in its reflection a figure resembling a female nurse, but adorned in Victorian clothing, was standing directly behind him. The woman wore a grim expression, which held Charles transfixed until he shook himself away from the ashen glare.

Mr Bide scampered out of the building. He spoke of his encounter with a doctor, but due to the pressures of the war, there was no time for the doctor to investigate his claim. However, it is alleged that for a few years after Charles' experience, many others came forward to report the phantom, but none of their confrontations were as chilling as Mr Bide's.

Greenwich Ghouls

Several decades ago, author Elliot O'Donnell recorded many famous and obscure apparitions in his books. On 24 July 1898, the writer claimed to have had a weird encounter with a 'nature spirit', as he described it, while he was perched on a bench in Greenwich Park. O'Donnell was shadowed by the diseased branches of an elm tree, when suddenly something caught his eye, a form which fell from the tree. It was no mere leaf, piece of rotten bark or insect, but a creature half-human, half-animal, '… stunted, bloated, pulpy and yellow', which, as it hit the floor, moved sideways like a crab and headed off towards a bush. O'Donnell fled the park, disturbed by the thing he'd seen.

In 1966 Revd R.N. Hardy took a photograph of not just one, but two spirits while at the Queen's House, National Maritime Museum. The picture showed a figure on the Tulip staircase, it resembled a monk in its dark garb and was hooded. It appeared to be walking up the stairs, its left arm resting on the bannister. In front of the monk-like spectre is the arm of another, less discernible spook. Investigations at the time into the possibility of a haunting resulted in footsteps being heard, but nothing seen.

The Royal Naval College at Greenwich also has a ghost. Author Peter Underwood mentioned such a ghoul in the Queen Anne Block, which was reported on 1 January 1962, when a Mr Edward C. Hull and a colleague noticed a door handle violently rattle and the door thrown open. Footsteps and tapping sounds were also reported.

Some believe the ghost to be of Admiral Byng, who was imprisoned in the college in 1757, before his execution for treason.

Strangeness at Stockwell

The case of the Stockwell Poltergeist has been pretty much forgotten, mainly because it took place in 1772, but it deserves a resurrection for it remains a chilling yarn.

The phenomenon centred upon a Mrs Golding at her farmhouse. Although the beginnings of the case suggested nothing more than a nuisance spirit that occasionally threw plates from the wall, something sinister was on the cards one particular day when Mrs Golding fainted. Aided by the local doctor, the woman recovered but had begun to bleed, and so she was rushed to the sink where, in amazement, they both stood and watched as the blood began to spring from the sink, and the basin shattered before them.

Every time guests were welcomed into the house by the owner, they were offered a glass of wine or rum, but the glasses in which they were served smashed one by one, and at dinner joints of meat would fly into the air and tumultuous noises would resonate throughout the house as if the building were about to collapse. The children of the house were terrified by the unseen presence and were rushed to a local barn by the maid, Ann Robinson, but whether by coincidence or eerie reasoning, the activity stopped once the maid was gone.

Green Park.

Peace at last resumed in the house, but when Miss Robinson returned all hell broke loose. Beer casks of considerable weight were tossed into the air, candlesticks thrown at the wall and a bucket of cold water began to boil suddenly. Seeing sense, or maybe as a last resort, Mrs Golding fired the maid and the uproar ceased, leaving the farmhouse as still as the night.

The Haunted Tree

It is said that St James's Hospital for Leprous Women used the site now known as Green Park as a burial ground for victims, and a strange legend now centres upon the park.

This story revolves around a particular tree in the vicinity. It has become known as the 'tree of death', and no bird is said to perch on its branches, let alone sing in its shadow. Dog-walkers claim that their pets avoid the tree and those who have experienced its sinister aura state that while in the shade of the tree, they are overcome by a feeling of overwhelming sadness. The most peculiar quality of the tree, or whatever lurks within its aged bark, is its ability to omit an eerie gurgling sound, as if someone is trapped within the tree and gasping for air.

Could these bizarre noises be connected to the sinister black figure said to have been sighted beside the tree? This malevolent apparition exudes menace and many witnesses have commented that the figure points at them and then vanishes into thin air.

Is there any truth in the belief that many have been found hanging from the tree in the past, and could such tragedy be locked within the tree as some kind of dormant energy? Whatever the truth behind this tree, one thing is sure, unless someone stays the night under its creaking bows, the legend will remain until proven otherwise. Naturally, the tale has become something of an urban legend, although no one actually knows which tree exactly is meant to be haunted!

The Policeman who Saved a Ghost

Despite the hidden alleyways, dark crevices and secret crannies of the city, it comes as a surprise that the area around Cleopatra's Needle, on the Victoria Embankment, remains one of the most haunted. The Needle, brought to the capital in 1878, stands on the banks of the River Thames like some sky-puncturing watcher, and, if such an obelisk had eyes, it would have seen many a tragedy.

This specific location is known for many suicides, more than any other stretch of the river. During the 1940s a peculiar encounter involving a policeman took place in the vicinity. One foggy night the officer was approached by a woman who hysterically told him that a lady was about to leap into the cold, grey waters of the Thames. She frantically motioned to the policeman to follow her to the spot, and, as they arrived at Cleopatra's Needle, he could clearly see a woman about to jump from the bridge. The policeman lunged for the despondent soul, wrenching her back to safety, but received the shock of his life. There before him stood the same woman he could have sworn only seconds ago had warned him of the pending tragedy. The policeman looked around him, but there was no woman to be seen.

Some people have reported that on dark, mist-enshrouded nights, eerie moans can be heard near the Needle; others believe that the groans are emanating from within the granite form itself. On several occasions there have been sightings of a naked figure, running across the riverside terrace and plunging into the murky depths. This is always a silent event, with no screaming, no sound of padding feet or even splash of water, and never any sign below that a person is flailing amidst the racing waves.

Apparitions of Monks at Acton

Alongside white and grey ladies, the monk has to be one of the most symbolic of ghostly legends around Britain. Such figures signify the peace and tranquillity of old abbeys and priorys, as they walk or glide, like shadows, adorned in their cowls, along ancient pathways flanked by ruinous walls.

Apparitions of monks haunt Acton.

Acton is not exactly London's most haunted location, but, in the vicinity of St Dunstan's Church at East Acton, a whole procession of hooded figures has been seen heading towards a wall, into which they disappear. No one really knows why they haunt the area, but author John Harries, in his *The Ghost Hunter's Road Book*, wrote:

> These ghosts are of too recent an origin for any traditional story to explain their haunting. Until a century ago it was a small village and noted for the piety of its inhabitants. In the seventeenth century it was a centre of Puritanical zeal; possibly the phantom monks were the victims of persecution of their order.

St Bartholomew the Great is one of the oldest churches in the capital. What's left of the priory was founded by a monk named Rahere, who is also said to have founded the adjacent hospital. It is believed to be his ghost that loiters in the grounds, particularly around his own tomb and effigy. Other researchers disagree and claim that the monk phantom is a martyr who was burned in the area of Smithfield, not far from the church.

In the Shadow of the Ripper

Although the environment which once harboured the elusive Jack the Ripper has altered a great deal since 1888, his ghastly crimes have no doubt left an indelible mark upon the framework of the buildings. In the annals of London folklore there is no greater enigma than the shadowy presence of this maniac, who, over the course of his reign slayed five, or maybe more victims. Despite constant speculation and investigation, Jack the Ripper remains one of the most intriguing serial killers to have ever prowled this planet, and the echoes of his crimes can still be heard today.

Do Jack the Ripper's victims still haunt Whitechapel?

Hanbury Street, where Annie Chapman was killed and possibly still haunts.

Miller's Court, Spitalfields, was the setting for Jack's most barbaric kill, that of Mary Jane Kelly, who was mutilated beyond recognition. The room (No. 13, Miller's Court) no longer exists, but on occasion it has been reported that Mary Jane has been sighted in the vicinity. Adorned in black, she wanders the night.

Famous ghost-hunters Elliot O'Donnell and Peter Underwood reported on the ghosts of Ripper victims Lizzie Stride (third victim) and Catherine Eddowes (fourth victim). O'Donnell mentioned that a week after the grisly throat-cutting of Stride (whose body was found 30 September 1888 in a yard beside No. 40 Berner Street), a local business man was unnerved by several moans coming from the shadows. Knocking on a door to enquire what the noise was, he was told by a woman in the street, 'It's no good knocking there guv'nor. Them sounds don't come from that 'ouse. They're in the street 'ere. We've often 'eard them since poor Lizzie Stride was done to death.'

At Mitre Square, where Catherine Eddowes was found disembowelled (throat also cut, left kidney and uterus excised and taken away), there have been several reports of a female figure huddled in what became known as 'Ripper's corner'.

Annie Chapman was killed in Hanbury Street; her body found behind No. 29 on 8 September 1888. Her throat had been so severely cut that the head was almost severed. There have been reports of strange moans and also a headless figure in this area. With so much blood spilled at Whitechapel, it's no surprise that the victims are still said to wander in limbo the alleyways and dark corners. The only question is, have they found peace, or does the spectre of the Ripper continue to haunt them, just as he continues to haunt the avenues and alleyways of London folklore?

EIGHT

MISCELLANEOUS MYSTERIES

Supernatural Swarms?

On 2 April 1902 it was said that an unnatural darkness fell upon Wimbledon. The shadow hadn't been caused by smoke or clouds and locals began to panic considerably until, after ten minutes, the eeriness subsided. Had the residents of this London suburb been besieged by a swarm of insects? Cases of such have been numerous across the capital.

Twenty years later the Surrey suburbs of London were, according to authors John Michell and Bob Rickard, '… afflicted by swarms of small stinging flies like a mosquito with spotted wings.' However, entomologist Professor H.M. Lefroy could not identify the insect. At the time a plague of ladybirds had also gathered over London and Kent. However, the biggest swarm recorded was in the 1800s, when a huge dark cloud of millions of unidentified insects was seen moving over Battersea. At first, as the shadow loomed over the area, residents had thought that it was smoke billowing from the tree tops.

The early ladybird invasions provoked much debate among entomologists, who stated, at a meeting in London, that the swarms consisted of insects far bigger than those seen previously in the UK. Sailors and fishermen aboard boats in the Channel were docking covered in these extraordinary masses. The *London Standard* of 20 August 1869 commented that the ladybirds were '… of a paler colour with more spots'.

The year 1974 saw one of the most severe swarms, when caterpillars of the Vapourer moth invaded Berkeley Square and completely covered a statue. The *Sunday Times* reported on the extraordinary swarm, stating:

> … the pestilence of caterpillars, as Westminster City Council calls it, arrived two weeks ago. Thousands of small furry creatures dropped 40ft from the square's plane trees. Some dropped on to passers-by, others fell on the statue of the topless Greek lady.

The head of London Zoo's insect house believed the insects may well have been drawn to the location because of the street lights. A local gardener took it upon himself to clean up the insects but gave up after a short while as more and more seemed to appear out of nowhere.

A London woman commented at the time that the invasion echoed a similar bout twenty years previously, at a Park Lane school. She also recalled caterpillars at Berkeley Square before, which people, completely unaware of, used to sit on as they rested on park benches. The insects were so dense in mass that locals probably never realised such creatures were present until they began to wriggle!

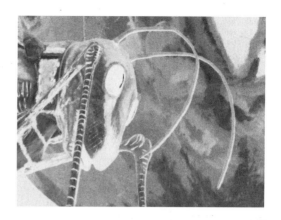

London has been plagued by bizarre,
supernatural insect swarms over the years.

A paranormal tale pertaining to a swarm emerged from 1797 in Hammersmith. The story revolves around a lady named Frances Murdoch, the wife of Mr Patrick Murdoch. They were a couple said to live on a pittance, although Frances did like a few glasses of stout and was prone to be rather loud when drunk. On 15 August 1797 Frances had been to the local inn with her husband. Frances had sat with several friends downing drink after drink and having a merry night, when one of her friends began to tell her about the problems she was having with a neighbour. According to Mrs Murdoch's friend, the next-door neighbour had a rather active beehive in the garden at Lillie Road. So, Frances, fuelled by alcohol, was hastily out of her chair and on a mission to help her friend out. She and her two drunken pals marched to the neighbour's garden. Once there, Frances proceeded to stumble and crash through the garden in an attempt to set free the bees and destroy the troublesome hive. Of course, the noise awoke the owner of the hive, who quickly came downstairs to confront the vandals on her property. She grabbed hold of Frances by her clothes and Frances retaliated by punching her full in the face, breaking two of her teeth.

Tragically, after the fracas, it seems that the lady who owned the garden died of a heart attack as she was found dead on her garden lawn the next day. Murdoch and her friends were traumatised by what they'd done and so eventually went to see the police to tell them that the hive had been a menace and that the woman was asked to get rid of it. They stated also that the woman had promised to get rid of the bees and so they left. The bruised face of the dead woman would have been a mystery to the police, however, it seems that they simply wanted the case solved and so noted that maybe the deceased had fallen on to the hive while trying to destroy it, injured herself and died of shock. It seemed as if it was case closed.

However, three weeks after the tragedy, the cousin of the deceased (a Hester Cecil) arrived from Ireland in the hope of sorting out the financial affairs of her relative. While looking through some old documents, Hester found that it had been noted on several occasions that Mrs Murdoch's friend, the neighbour of the deceased, had in fact threatened and hit the woman. This angered Hester, a strapping six-footer, who quickly stormed around to the neighbour's and banged on the door looking for answers. When the neighbour opened the door, Hester rushed in armed with a wooden club. The neighbour's husband confronted her but she was quick to strike him with the object and then lash out at his wife. Hester battered the couple with the club and then suddenly ceased, went out into the back garden and began a strange

A swarm of bees was conjured up at Hammersmith as an act of revenge.

dance and chant. Suddenly many bees began to circle Hester, but not to sting her, as if they were under her command. The hundreds of bees became a huge swarm that formed a black cloud. Hester then stopped her jig, outstretched her arms and screamed into the air, 'Frances Murdoch!'

Suddenly, the bees moved away and began to travel *en masse* along the road, where they sought out the home of Frances Murdoch. The woman was just about to leave for the butcher's shop when she was buzzed by the thousands of insects. As she attempted a scream, her mouth was filled by the swarm, as were her nostrils and ears. Her whole body was covered by the bees and in ten minutes Frances Murdoch was dead on the pavement, her body swollen and deformed by the thousands of stings inflicted by the angry bees apparently commanded by Hester Cecil in revenge for the killing of her cousin.

Legend has it that Hester was charged with assault but she returned to Ireland without facing prosecution.

Another swarm of bees converged at Hammersmith in 1877, when an early suffragette march in support of contraceptive campaigner Annie Besant were buzzed by the insects. Strangely, despite the huge number of bees, no one was stung and not one bee was found dead or injured by the attempted swipes from the crowd.

In 1936, also at Hammersmith, a protest march of over 300 people who were carrying placards reading 'We Want King Edward VIII', was bombarded by a huge swarm of seemingly supernatural bees. One woman commented, 'I was lashing out with my placard, but it seemed to go straight through them. I really can't understand it!'

The Freak Storm

It was like a scene from a blockbuster disaster movie in the end, but how it all began was a mystery. The *Kentish Mercury* and *Kentish Independent* of 24 July were both on hand to record the storm of 21 and 22 July 1925 which swept through Eltham, Woolwich, Plumstead and Shooters Hill and then on to Erith and Bexleyheath.

It had been the hottest afternoon for two years, reaching 90 degrees Fahrenheit. The humidity rose and thunder began to rumble around 5 p.m. – this was no real surprise, but the bizarre weather which accompanied the claps of thunder shocked the eastern half of the capital. Firstly there was torrential rain and by 6 p.m. the streets were flooded; buses and fire engines were stranded in the middle of torrents of water which swept through the roads. Lightning reached from the heavens, striking buildings – and then came the ice. No one had seen anything like it before, pounding hailstones that reached the size of eggs crashed onto vehicles and shattered windows. Some of these jagged spikes measured up to four inches. Lawns were turned white in minutes as the tornado-like force swept through upper Plumstead, hammering pedestrians for ten minutes, the vicious shards cutting flesh and ripping clothing.

Such was the severity of the hail that birds were killed as they sat sheltering in trees, and fields of cows and horses were turned to chaos as bewildered animals ran to avoid the storm.

One of the hailstones found at Abbey Wood weighed 10½oz, and at Woolwich one weighed over a pound; huge lumps of ice were discovered at Eltham and the Conservative Club at Belvedere had a six-inch hole in its roof made by one giant piece of ice.

In January 1975, Fulham Road was bombarded by hailstones allegedly weighing 50lb. Flats at Fulham Court were severely damaged during the fall and tiles were smashed to smithereens. During August of the same year hail as big as marbles descended upon Hampstead, while according to reports some three million tons of water hit the North London suburb.

Fish from the Sky

A strange thing happened one autumn evening in 1893. On Kensington High Street, a young gentleman was taking his usual stroll home from a hard day at work when, upon reaching Kensington Church Street, he suddenly received a blow to the head. The man hadn't been robbed of any possessions, and no one had seen the attacker, except one witness who rushed to the man's aid, carrying him to a nearby house before the hospital visit. The witness had bizarre news for the victim. He hadn't been accosted by a sinister criminal, but in fact had been struck by … a fish! Upon arriving at the scene the witness spotted the silvery form, a roach in fact (a common freshwater fish), lying by the side of the man. The witness, upon helping the man to his feet, noticed several fish scales dotted around his shoulder where the fish had struck. The news of the weird encounter spread like wildfire and soon the press were eager to run the headline of the flying fish – the story became even more peculiar when it was discovered that the gentleman who had been dealt such a blow was in fact named Mr Chub, the name of another freshwater fish!

A local professor of zoology stated that the fish had most probably been dropped by a bird, such as a seagull or heron. Whatever the case, the injured chap staggered to his feet and made his way home for tea, praying deep down that his wife hadn't prepared him chips with a nice lump of fish. Battered of course.

During 1975, shortly after a storm at Hampstead, a man discovered a West African python on his window ledge after the heavy rainfall. The creature was carted off to London Zoo.

On 26 May 1984, a Mr Ron Langton was enjoying some late-night television at his home in East Ham when he was unsettled by a peculiar noise outside. It sounded for all the world as if his roof was being hit every few minutes or so, and by something which slapped as it

Across London fish have been recorded as falling from the sky.

Model of a roach
Rutilus rutilus
Europe to Asia

In 1893 a Kensington man was hit on the head by a roach which fell from the sky!

In 1921 dancing coals were recorded in several households across the capital.

made impact. The strange noise went on for quite a few minutes but Ron was too relaxed to go outside and take a look. The next morning he was amazed to find six fish scattered on his roof and lawn. The fish measured approximately 12cm long and appeared to be flounders and whiting.

A more extreme fish fall was record at Canning Town, where two witnesses discovered some forty fish strewn about the gardens. Theories put forward included a waterspout from the Thames lifting the fish, or seagulls dropping them, but the solutions seemed even more bizarre than the odd events.

In February 2004 people travelling on the Thames Bubbler boat at Dagenham were astonished when what appeared to be a piranha dropped from nowhere, and slapped onto the deck. The Environment Agency theorised that a seagull had dropped the fish, despite the piranha belonging to waters some 5,000 miles away in the murky depths of the Amazon. Those who observed the fish noticed that the beak marks of a gull were evident, but the only suggestion they could come up with as to why the fish had made its way to London, was as an import that was then discarded in the local waters, where it would have perished due to the cold.

The Case of the Dancing Coals

'There can be no doubt of the phenomena. I have seen them, myself', so said the Revd A.L. Gardiner in 1921 as London was hit by a mysterious mini-plague pertaining to the exploding of coal from grates. Ordinary enough, but it was not so simple to explain. Such pieces were then said to dance along the floor, especially in the home of a Mr J.S. Frost who reported in the January, at his residence of 8 Ferristone Road, Hornsey, that other, usually inanimate objects, such as ornaments, flat irons and coal buckets, also took on a life of their own.

These peculiar happenings were discussed at a local meeting on 8 May while sceptics argued that it was the three children of Mr Frost who must surely have toyed with the items. And yet the youngsters, namely Gordon, Bertie and Muriel, were quite terrified by the events to the extent that on 1 April Muriel died of shock, the story being covered by the *Daily Mail*.

Mr Frost's son Gordon was taken to Lewisham after a nervous breakdown, the family having been plagued by several incidents. The police were called to investigate after coal buckets began to explode, with showers of coals raining from nowhere in the house, as if they'd passed through walls to appear in several rooms. Additionally, despite violent falls to the ground, ornaments remained unbroken and a pot on a tripod was said to have swung aggressively while no person or wind caused it to shift.

A Dr Herbert Lemerle of Hornsey spoke of a clock that mysteriously vanished into thin air and even stranger was the fact that similar cases occurred around Europe, particularly France, Belgium and Switzerland, the only connection being that in all cases British coal was used. In 1921 a woman was killed in her Guildford home when coal exploded from the grate.

Author Charles Fort wrote, 'In this period there was much disaffection among British coal miners. There was a suspicion that miners were mixing dynamite into coal', although such rumours were proved wrong when checks were introduced. However, at the time it was easier to blame the miners than a poltergeist!

Phantom Stone Throwers

Unexplained cases pertaining to the sudden appearance of mystery objects from nowhere have, most certainly in the past, been blamed on the poltergeist, or 'noisy ghost' – an unseen phantom energy said to throw objects and make others appear. On 27 April 1872 the *London Times* reported on a strange incident in Bermondsey:

> From 4 p.m. (Thursday) to 11 p.m., the houses 56 and 58 Reverdy Road were assailed with stones and other missiles coming from an unseen quarter. Two children were injured, every window broken, and several articles of furniture were destroyed. Although there was a strong body of policemen scattered in the neighbourhood, they could not trace the direction from where the stones were thrown.

Pennies from Heaven

A shower of coins was said to have rained down on Trafalgar Square in the 1800s, causing a great commotion as hundreds of passers-by scrambled to grasp the rolling pennies. And such pennies from Heaven also appeared in Battersea, as reported in *New York Evening World* on 18 January 1928, but on this occasion the copper coins materialised indoors from nowhere, alongside large lumps of coal, leaving the residents, the Robinson family, perplexed.

In 1876 several 'thunderstones' fell upon London after severe weather conditions. The mysterious rocks, said to weigh around 8lbs, had been known to appear in various forms, often beautifully polished and green in colour; others resembled axes, made of flint.

In 1866 coal-like objects descended upon Notting Hill during late June. During this particularly heavy storm it was also reported that rain and hail poured from a clear sky! In June 1880 a large stone struck a house at Oakley Street in Chelsea. A theory was put forward that such an object had meteoric properties, but on 17 August 1887 a lump of roundish iron that clattered onto Brixton was not as easily explained. The object had fallen during another severe storm.

During the 1800s a shower of pennies was reported across London.

Symbols & Signs

On 15 November 1895, at 12 p.m., 'an alarming explosion' rocked the capital in an area near Fenchurch Street. However, this was no ordinary explosion, because, despite the violent blast, which caused hundreds of people to swarm the vicinity, there was in fact no evidence to suggest any impact. Terrified locals swore that buildings shook, debris flew and foundations creaked, and yet there were no destructive signs – it seemed as though the explosion was a phantom one!

It was rumoured that a handful of people, caught up in the panic, had seen 'something' fall from the sky, but the police could find no such object. Authorities suggested at the time that maybe some 'thing' had been placed in the street such as fog-signals which then exploded as vehicles passed. Eerily, at around the same time mysterious craft resembling airships had been observed over London. Were ghost ships dropping phantom bombs on the capital?

During 1966 in Walthamstow, many people flocked to a local church after a crucifix began to 'weep'. The strange crying lasted for more than ten weeks, leading many to believe that it was a sign of the Second Coming, while others feared that doom was coming to the capital. Of course, the bizarre theories dried up, along with the alleged tears, and London remains intact.

In 1832, as cholera swept the land, purging and vomiting was certainly the order of the day, but as some of those who suffered looked to the skies above London, they claimed to have seen a flaming sword. It was a sign, but a sign of what? A century later, a similar sign appeared in the sky, this time as the Crystal Palace burned. Witnesses spoke of a great red light in the Heavens, and the words that escaped their lips were of hope, for they believed that the old ways of the old world were over.

A Fairy Encounter?

What Jacqui Ford saw as a child has remained with her for over thirty years. At the time, in the 1970s, she was living at Manor Park in the London Borough of Newham. One morning as she stirred from slumber and glanced towards the bottom of the bed, she saw standing there a

Fenchurch Street, where a phantom explosion occurred.

creature … no, a human … around eight inches in height that looked just like the archetypal fairy. It was female, with blonde flowing hair, a silvery flimsy dress, transparent wings and holding what appeared to be a wand.

After a short time the small being walked across the bed and leapt towards the sink that Jacqui had in her room. The fairy then proceeded to disappear down the plug-hole, leaving Jacqui stunned by its presence. Certain that it was not a dream, she remained convinced that what she'd observed was the perfect specimen of a fairy that she thought only existed in fantasy.

Dracula Woz Ere!

If you found the legend of the Highgate Vampire too hard to swallow, consider this tale.

On 15 and 17 August 1978, the *London Evening News* reported on a rather bizarre discovery – the alleged grave of a vampire … well, not just any vampire, but the king of the undead, Count Dracula!

While renovations were underway at a house in Peckham, South London, workmen stumbled upon a peculiar slab of granite resembling a grave as they were burrowing in the soil. Even stranger was the inscription upon the surface, which read, 'Count Dracula, 17.12.1847'.

Had the builders uncovered some gothic chamber or eerie tomb lost to the world for over a century? Site agent James Davis seemed to think so. He told the press that while keeping watch one night for vandals, he became extremely spooked and his Doberman Pinscher dog was afraid to venture into the garden where the strange burial site has been found. Even the next-door neighbour, Mr Francis, got involved, stating, 'It's eerie. If they find any dead'uns in there, I'm moving out. Let alone undead'uns!'

After a few days of bemusement and chilled confusion, step forward former resident David Perrin to solve the riddle. It was he, he claimed, who thirteen years before, as a fifteen-year-old boy, had put the slab in the ground and carved the inscription. He did it for a joke, never realising it would be unearthed over a decade later to cause such bemusement.

So, no real vampires on this occasion to get our teeth into, but don't throw the garlic away just yet …

A Visit from the Devil

Mrs Maude M.C. Ffoulkes submitted a story to a volume called *Weird Stories* back in the early 1900s. She had a bizarre encounter in the autumn of 1916 while residing in flats at Curzon Street, Mayfair in the West End of the capital. At the time these were modern flats, although her residence incorporated the top floor of a house which originally stood at the entrance to an old inn. It was alleged that one of the small rooms was once used as a hiding place for Dick Turpin.

Mrs Ffoulkes stated at the time that her bedroom was very difficult to access for any would-be burglar's, but one Thursday night in October 1916 someone, or some 'thing', had intruded upon her property. She was awoken in the early hours by a presence. A young man was standing at the foot of the bed and staring intently at Maude.

'I have never forgotten his face; it was essentially grave, more or less Italian in type, peculiarly attractive and entirely unusual,' she said.

Maude sat bolt upright in bed and asked who the man was and what he wanted.

'I am the Devil,' he replied, 'and I have come to bargain with you for the souls of two people who have greatly wronged you. Their hatred is of such a quality that they are now delivered into your hands.'

Although Maude thought on impulse this was some random lunatic who'd broken in to her home, deep down she felt some kind of belief in his ominous words.

Then, she fell back to sleep. However, the same thing happened on the following Saturday. This time, however, Maude was brave enough to challenge the visitor, saying to him, 'There is no such thing as the Devil. He is a scriptual myth and a fearsome creation of medieval times. Goodness and sin are entirely mental attributes, and Lucifer is but an allegorical figure.'

The man promptly responded, 'You are entirely wrong. I exist and I shall always exist as visible "Evil" for those whose clear vision enables them to see me as you do now. Believe me, I am actually here – and tomorrow morning you will find indisputable proof of the truth of my words.'

On the Sunday morning Mrs Ffoulkes' maid brought in a cup of tea and passed to Maude her dressing gown. Immediately the maid moaned, 'Oh, what have you done to your shoulder?'

'Why nothing,' answered Maude, looking in the mirror only to see an image of a man's hand imprinted blue-black on the skin.

Despite discussing the incident with several friends, the strange man was never to return.

Strangers Beneath Our Feet

The London Underground worms its way through a large part of London, as well as slinking through neighbouring Essex, Buckinghamshire and Hertfordshire. Its first sections opened in 1863 and it now stretches for around 250 miles. Approximately 270 stations are dotted along the serpentine track, and in 2007 more than one billion journeys were recorded from the metro system. It is rumoured to be extremely haunted and a great book on the subject is *Haunted London Underground* by David Brandon and Alan Brooke. However, there are a

The dark tunnels of London Underground are said to be inhabited by a subterranean race.

couple of very weird mysteries often over-looked when it comes to the dark tunnels of the Underground.

In 1972 a British horror film called *Deathline*, also known as *Raw Meat*, was released. It concerns the urban myth that a race of cannibals exist under the streets of London, carrying out their acts of carnage on all manner of victims such as tramps, drunks, city workers and pets. Legend has it that they roam the sewers, the London Underground, railway tunnels and just about any black hole they can find to shelter and conceal themselves. They have their own guttural language and are known to be aggressive when encountered.

Folklorist Michael Goss looked into the possibility of any truth behind the legend and concluded that although primal or neglected humans may not be loitering in the underground, belief in such dwellers was once rife. He state that:

> They are not representatives of the desperate, homeless poor, nor are they thrill-seeking interlopers indulging in the frisson that comes from being where they are not supposed to be … the London subterranean are real troglodytes, born and bred down below and seldom if ever coming to the surface.

Of course, these secretive souls, who feed on the food we don't want as well as animals such as mice and rats – and, as some would have it, the occasional human victim – have never been sighted. Is that because they do not exist or because the London above them is completely oblivious to their existence?

The Monster In The Tunnels

Of all the weird phenomena pertaining to London, what you are about to read is possibly one of the strangest tales. This story comes via two reputable researchers – Jonathan Downes and Nick Redfern.

Nick, a Texas-based investigator and author, was contacted by Jonathan Downes (who runs The Centre for Fortean Zoology, the world's largest community in search of mythical and elusive beasts) regarding the rumour that during the 1940s a very bizarre creature was housed at the Royal Counties Hospital in Exeter.

Downes worked at the hospital as a nurse between 1982 and 1985 and recalled many tales about phone calls from Devonshire Police Force and the Lord Lieutenant of the county. These calls were in reference to a dangerous 'patient' who would be brought to the hospital. This patient was 6ft in height, like a very muscular man, but covered in hair. It was alleged that the patient was housed at the hospital for three days but was then transferred to an unspecified location beneath the London Underground.

No one knows what happened to the 'wild-man', but in the 1960s a Mr Campbell recalled that while travelling on the tube one evening he encountered what could well have been the monstrous entity. Mr Campbell stood at a deserted stop on the Northern Line when he heard a growl from behind him. When he turned he saw an ape-like beast heading towards the track. However, this beast, which resembled Bigfoot, seemed to be ghostly in nature because part of its body appeared to be merging with the concrete platform while the rest of it was above the ground.

One of London's strangest hauntings occurred on the London Underground. During the 1960s a witness observed an ethereal man-beast whilst travelling on the Northern Line. (Illustration by Adam Smith)

Such fears were brought to the big screen in 1981 when the movie *An American Werewolf in London* featured a salivating beast stalking the London Underground in search of victims. However, zoologist Richard Freeman dismissed the story as nothing more than a legend based upon a mental patient, and not a wild man.

SELECT BIBLIOGRAPHY

Books

Anon, *Strange Encounters* (Parragon, 2000)

Anon, *Weird Stories* (Illustrated Newspapers Ltd, 1928)

Arnold, Neil *Monster! The A-Z of Zooform Phenomena* (CFZ Press, 2007)

Arnold, Neil *Mystery Animals of the British Isles – Kent* (CFZ Press, 2009)

Bondeson, Jan *The London Monster* (Da Capo Press, 2002)

Brandon, David & Brooke, Alan *Haunted London Underground* (The History Press, 2009)

Brooks, J.A. *Ghosts of London* (Jarrold, 1995)

Chambers, Michael *Chambers' Guide to London, the Secret City* (Ocean, 1975)

Collins, Andrew *The Brentford Griffin* (Earthquest, 1985)

Cobbett, William *Rural Rides* (Constable, 1982)

Farrant, David *Beyond the Highgate Vampire* (B.P.O.S., 1991)

Fort, Charles *Wild Talents* (John Brown, 1998)

Haining, Peter *The Legend and Bizarre Crimes of Spring-Heeled Jack* (Muller, 1977)

Harries, John *The Ghost Hunter's Road Book* (Muller, 1968)

Jones, Richard & Coe, Chris *Haunted London* (New Holland, 2004)

Lazarus, Richard *Beyond the Impossible* (Warner, 1994)

Lee, Revd F.G. *Glimpses in the Twilight* (Edinburgh, 1885)

Maple, Eric *The Realm of Ghosts* (Pan, 1964)

Matthews, Marcus *Big Cats Loose in Britain* (CFZ Press, 2007)

Michell, John & Rickard, Robert J.M. *Living Wonders* (Thames & Hudson, 1982)

O'Donnell, Elliot, *Casebook of Ghosts* (Nel, 1971)

O'Donnell, Elliot *Dangerous Ghosts* (Consul, 1954)

O'Donnell, Elliot *Haunted Britain* (Rider, 1952)

Robson, Alan *Nightmare on Your Street: More Grisly Trails and Ghostly Tales* (Virgin, 1993)

Shuker, Dr Karl P.N. *From Flying Toads to Snakes with Wings* (Llewellyn, 1997)

Watson, Nigel *The Scareship Mystery* (Domra, 2000)

Newspapers & Magazines

Daily Mail

Daily Mirror

Daily Telegraph

Evening Standard

Field Magazine

Fortean Times

Guardian

Hampstead & Highgate Express

Kensington Express

Kentish Independent

Kentish Mercury

Kentish Times

Land & Water

London Morning Post

London Times

Magonia

Mayfair

Newsshopper

New York Evening World

Review of Reviews

Rochester Gazette & Weekly Advertiser

Southwark News

Sun

Sunday Dispatch

Sunday Times

Suspended In Dusk

The Gentleman's Magazine

The Job

West London Observer

Wimbledon Guardian

Websites

www.bbc.co.uk

www.beastsoflondon.blogspot.com

www.kentbigcats.blogspot.com

www.paranormaldatabase.com

www.roadghosts.com

www.spicycauldron.com

www.thamesangel.com

www.thisislocallondon

www.UFOinfo.com

Other local titles published by The History Press

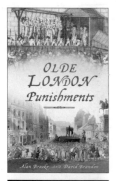

Olde London Punishments

ALAN BROOKE & DAVID BRANDON

Over the centuries, many hundreds have expired inside the capital's dank, rat-infested cells, or whilst 'dancing the Tyburn jig' at the end of a swinging rope, and many of the sites in this book have become bywords for infamy. From the Tower and Newgate prison to the Clink and the Fleet, this book explores London's criminal heritage. Also including the stocks and pillories that lie, almost forgotten, in churchyards and squares across the City, and the many shocking punishments exacted inside the region's churches, workhouses and schools, it is a heart-breaking survey of our nation's penal history.

978 0 7524 5456 6

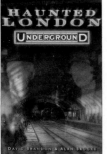

Haunted London Underground

DAVID BRANDON & ALAN BROOKE

This chilling book reveals well-known and hitherto unpublished tales of spirits, spectres and other spooky occurrences on one of the oldest railway networks in the world. The stories include the ghost of an actress regularly witnessed on Aldywch Station, the 'Black Nun' at Bank Station and the cries of thirteen-year-old Anne Naylor, who was murdered in 1758 near to the site of what is now Farringdon Station. These and many more ghostly accounts are recorded in fascinating detail in this book, which is a must-read for anyone interested in the mysterious and murky history of London's Underground.

978 0 7524 4746 9

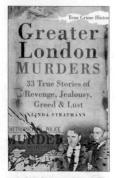

Greater London Murders: 33 True Stories of Revenge, Jealousy, Greed & Lust

LINDA STRATMANN

Greater London has been home to some of the most shocking murders in England. Contained within the pages of this book are the stories behind these heinous crimes. They include George Chapman, who was hanged in 1903 for poisoning three women, and whom is widely suspected of having been the notorious serial killer Jack the Ripper; and Donald Hume, who was found not guilty of the murder of wealthy businessman Stanley Setty in 1949, but later confessed to killing him, chopping up his body and disposing of it by aeroplane.

978 0 7524 5124 4

Paranormal Surrey

RUPERT MATTHEWS

In this volume, well-known local author Rupert Matthews, an expert on the subject of the paranormal, draws together a terrifying and intriguing collection of first-hand accounts and long-forgotten archive reports from the county's history. From big cat sightings and ancient monsters to poltergeists and UFOs, this compendium of the bizarre events that have shocked and frightened the residents of Surrey is richly illustrated with a range of modern photographs and archive images.

978 0 7524 5422 1

Visit our website and discover thousands of other History Press books.

www.thehistorypress.co.uk